Kama Sense Marketing

A Love Affair with Your Customers

Jacob Levy

iUniverse, Inc.
New York   Bloomington

Kama Sense Marketing
A Love Affair with Your Customers

iUniverse books may be ordered through booksellers or by contacting:

iUniverse
1663 Liberty Drive
Bloomington, IN 47403
www.iuniverse.com
1-800-Authors (1-800-288-4677)

Because of the dynamic nature of the Internet, any Web addresses or links contained in this book may have changed since publication and may no longer be valid.

ISBN: 978-1-4401-9556-3 (sc)
ISBN: 978-1-4401-9554-9 (dj)
ISBN: 978-1-4401-9555-6 (ebk)

Printed in the United States of America

iUniverse rev. date: 5/3/2010

Love is where physical, emotional, and spiritual experiences meet for the purpose of strengthening relationships.

—*The Complete Idiot's Guide to the Kama Sutra*

Isn't this what marketing is all about?

Contents

Introduction

"I love Coca-Cola."
"I love the way Estée Lauder products feel on my skin."
"I love shopping at Bloomies."
"I am in love with my Mac."

As a marketing practitioner and a researcher, I've known for quite some time that female consumers bring emotionality and passion into their relationships with their favorite brands. In turn, they want their favorite brands to woo and love them. Furthermore, women—in focus groups or among friends—freely use *love* to describe their feelings toward their favorite company, store, or brand.

In a recent evaluative study on cell phone company service, a young woman recounted the wonderful treatment and attention she had received from her service provider after complaining about a serious mistake the company had made on her bill. This woman did not hesitate to describe her relationship with the organization in romantic terms. When describing the treats and gifts the company had sent her, she remarked, somewhat jokingly, "This company treated me better than my husband."

And the theme gets even more provocative: A recent TV documentary showed a young woman in her twenties with a tattoo of Apple computer on her leg. She bragged, "I never have, nor will I ever, go to bed with a guy who uses Windows."

Yet marketers rarely, if ever, use *love* to describe how they feel about their customers. Instead, companies refer to the rather sterile "emotional relationship." In Israel, the cell phone operator Orange (part of the Hong Kong Hutchison Whampoa Limited Group) defines its customers' service experience with these one-word emotional benefits, posted on their service center walls: *Enjoy, play, together, future, relax, explore, happy, fun, look, touch, create,* and *smile*—all without mentioning the emotional benefit, *love*.

Why are customers able—without any inhibition—to use the term *love* to describe their feelings toward brands and corporations, while companies themselves do not? Why do corporations play around with the art of love without calling it by its real name?

Is Emotional Marketing the Answer?

Over the past decade, I have watched with great interest as "emotional marketing" has replaced the traditional USP (unique selling proposition) created by Rover Reeves from Ted Bates in the '40s.

Functional differentiation. Originally, the USP was mostly a functional or physically oriented concept. For decades, companies struggled to give their customers better-quality products. Physical satisfaction born of new technology was the main reason for choosing one product over another (e.g., the

> **Physical Satisfaction born of new technology was the main reason for choosing one product over another.**

secret formula of Coca-Cola, the cool stripes of Aquafresh toothpaste). These products' unique features became the attributes that differentiated the product from others in consumers' eyes. But soon all competitors had the same technology, making it increasingly difficult to differentiate products based merely on the physical or functional.

Service-based differentiation. Companies then began to compete for the highest quality and the fastest speed of their service response rate—for example, the unique service of Nordstrom department store, which became a legend in the industry. Shortly after the introduction of their services, all cell phone competitors had similar network technologies and handsets. To ensure customer loyalty, competitors began to invest in better service centers, where they could exercise the human and personal touch. One service center manager bragged to me about an electronic screen on the wall showing the length of the telephone queue, concluding with shining eyes, "What can't be measured can't be reduced." He felt that his measuring system gave him unique capabilities for shortening his queuing and for better service to his clients.

Emotional differentiation. When all the competitors learned to offer the same efficient call center personal service, they had to look for other differentiating factors. This brought them to emotional positioning through their advertising and packaging, trying to convey warm relationships and emotions between the customer and the brand. Marketers realized that emphasizing the brand's emotional benefits could boost profits not just by creating product differentiation but even more so by creating loyal customers—all they had to do was add satisfying emotional experiences to tangible benefits.

> The emotional paradigm opened the gate to a paradise of creativity.

The advertising and creative people were the first to jump on the emotional bandwagon, producing provocative campaigns promoting seduction, temptation, and passion. Seminars, lectures, books, and articles were suddenly chock-full of talk about emotions. Consequently, the last decade could be classified as the proliferation of emotional marketing. The emotional paradigm opened the gate to a paradise of creativity.

From floating to fond memories. As stated in the brand's Web site, Ivory soap offers much more than a gentle, baby-smooth clean. Ivory was originally known for its ability to float in water—a functional differentiation. But nearly one hundred years later, the company began touting the Ivory girl, whose fresh face and skin testified to the purity of this simple, basic soap. Promoting the Ivory girl demonstrated emotional differentiation, bringing home the concept of "pure fun with Ivory." The classic Ivory name offers rich memories of a simpler time when fun was a daily event.

Limitations of emotional marketing. Emotional marketing, although new, is not enough. Although marketers are now thinking about how their customers feel about their product, emotional marketing is seen only as a precondition for achieving different kinds of consumer loyalty, defined by such terms as *engagement, relationship,* or *commitment.* Once marketers and advertisers began borrowing terminology from the emotional dictionary—*pleasure, desire, temptation, seduction, sensuality,* and even *passion*—they entered the Temple of Love through

> Once [they] began borrowing terminology from the emotional dictionary...they entered the Temple of Love through the back door.

the back door. Yet isn't emotional marketing missing the one emotion that could make it great? What about love? And what about reciprocity—that is, what about how marketers feel about their customers?

I was especially baffled by this omission in the new books that invoked "emotional marketing" and spawned a plethora of theories. Marc Gobe's *Emotional Branding: The New Paradigm for Connecting Brands to People* and Martin Landstrom's *Brand*

Sense: Build Powerful Brands through Touch, Taste, Smell, Sight, and Sound. These works, although full of discussions on passion, sensuality, and emotional attraction, don't talk at all about love as a dominant subject. In fact, the term love does not appear in their indexes even once.

Emotional marketing alone is like sex. Sex without love can be great, a true physical release. But think how good sex can be if it comes with love—using and enjoying both physical and emotional attributes of the same brand.

Love Has No Rules; It Is an Instinct

There could be three reasons for not using love more frequently in marketing:

1. They don't teach us in school about love, whether in the marketing world or in the real world.

2. Men are reluctant to use the word *love.*

3. Marketers and businesspeople lack a theory of love and are therefore reluctant to use terminology not backed up by theory.

Searching for a theory of love would not help. Three respected scientists—Lewis, Amini, and Lannon, in *A General Theory of Love*—have recently concluded that: "The adventure of seeking a theory of love is far from over … the heart's castle still hangs high in the heavens, shrouded in scudding clouds and obscured by mist. (230)"

Love is an ancient instinct and should be used so in life as well as in marketing. The best marketers are those who are the first to deploy their instincts. In fact, the whole concept of emotional marketing hinges on the use of instincts and intuitions rather than on rules. And one of the oldest and most common instincts in the world, second only to the survival instinct, is the instinct for love. So it seems only natural that marketers should use the love instinct to achieve their aims. And yet they rarely do. Why?

Unwilling to give up, and troubled by the fact that marketers ignore love both in philosophy and in practice, I probed a little deeper. In the absence of a theory, I decided to look for an appropriate analogy between romantic love and marketing. With a decision to look for ancient or sacred analogies with romantic love, I dug through Plato, Socrates, *The Perfumed Garden,* and finally, the *Kama Sutra.*

In my search, I drew encouragement from the much-quoted research showing that U.S. women participate in and influence 85 percent of all purchasing decisions in the family—on the other hand, 85 percent of all marketers are men!* Don't we have here some sort of analogy with romantic love, where the marketer (mostly male) is the wooer and the customer (mostly female) is the wooed?

This is how I got to the original *Kama Sutra.*

Kama Sutra Find

The Kama Sutra *is a breviary of love valid for all times and places*
(6)

I was more than thrilled to discover that the *Kama Sutra,* the ancient Indian love manual, was exactly what I was looking for. The *Kama Sutra*'s 530 pages were dedicated solely to explaining the philosophy, theory, practices, and arts of love. In this ancient society each gender could initiate the act of love and had the right to develop and express his or her emotional, physical, and

---

*   Advertising Age as quoted in "She means business" by Grant J. Schneider Time Inc P15, P22

spiritual needs without any cultural inhibitions or restrictions. Women were completely free to demand and receive love and satisfaction. Love was considered a positive and essential element of life; it was taught to elementary school children, who in ancient India learned the *Kama Sutra*'s sixty-four arts of love—practices that were not permitted throughout the Dark Ages and up to the middle of the twentieth century.

The *Kama Sutra* was written in the fourth century CE as a brief summary of theories and practices existing in oral form centuries before that. This ancient Hindu text was written in Sanskrit by Vatsyayana, a Hindu monk living in ancient India. Tradition holds that the author was a celibate scholar who lived sometime between the first and fourth centuries CE, probably during the great cultural flowering of the Gupta period.

Kama Sutra is not about pornography. In modern Western society, the *Kama Sutra* has become a synonym for creative sexual positions. In a recent lecture on my *Kama Sutra* marketing philosophy, I asked the audience who thought the original *Kama Sutra* included any picture or illustration. Half of the audience raised their hands. Yet, the original *Kama Sutra* had not even one single illustration in its 530 pages. In fact, only 20 percent of the original text is about sexual positions. The majority of the book is about philosophy and theory of love. *Kama* is literally love, desire, pleasure, sex. *Sutra* signifies a treatise, a thread, or discourse threaded on a series of aphorisms. *Sutra* was a standard term for a technical text.

This book uses quotes from Alain Danielou's translation of *The Complete Kama Sutra: The First Unabridged Modern Translation of the Classic Indian Text* (published by Park Street Press), a book which I highly recommend reading.

In his introduction, the translator states that: *"The Kama Sutra is not a pornographic work. It is merely an impartial and systematic study of one of the essential aspects of existence."* (4)

From *Kama Sutra* to *Kama Sense Marketing*

"The Kama Sutra *emphasizes relationship in its wholeness, not just its physical aspects. The* Kama Sutra *appeals to our desire for connection and deep intimacy as well as sexual satisfaction. It addresses our desire to be seen, appreciated, accepted, revered, and adored. And it addresses our spiritual hunger"* (13).

The *Kama Sutra* is about pleasing your partner even more than pleasing yourself. I hope all marketers one day will adopt the same philosophy in their daily business life. This book opens many doors for doing so. It synchronizes the philosophy of receiving with the philosophy of giving pleasure to your partner, regardless of gender, two philosophies that the Western world has not fully adopted until today.

The ancient Hindu culture believed in the integration of religion with sex. Passionate love in this world would lead to eternal bliss in the next. The *Kama Sutra* explores sexuality and love as an integral part of human existence. Arguing that happiness and moral duty depend upon elaborate social rituals to satisfy the essential needs of life, the *Kama Sutra*'s main emphasis is on how a person may best attract a member of the opposite sex and fulfill him or her physically and how this is a basic, essential aspect of human life.

The point of the *Kama Sutra* is to meld the physical, emotional, and spiritual aspects of love in a way that strengthens and expands relationships. In my opinion, there isn't a better definition for modern marketing. Aren't marketers interested in producing physical and emotional experiences for the purpose of strengthening their relationships with their customers?

The *Kama Sutra* is the most complete, holistic manual of wisdom and common sense on the philosophy and practice of love ever written. The *Kama Sutra* helps us easily apply the theories and practices of wooing between men and women to the relationship between a marketing manager and his or her customers. Consulting the ancient text of the *Kama Sutra* yields four distinct advantages for marketers:

1. It provides ancient wisdom and techniques that were practiced for generations in an unprecedented liberal society.

2. It recognizes the importance of women in love as both receiver and giver.

3. It enables a *new* marketing approach based on vocabulary that is familiar to both genders.

4. It provides triggers for endless creativity.

It's up to each marketer to peruse the *Kama Sutra*, discover the analogies, consider the tactics, and use them for his purposes.

Putting all these concepts together in one coherent whole is new. This new perspective on the relationship between a company and its clients can pave the way for many new and creative marketing approaches and concepts that were never previously considered. Like in the *Kama Sutra*, I believe that the female consumer wants her favorite brands to woo and love her. And I look to the *Kama Sutra* to learn how this can best be achieved. This creed for complete reciprocity captures a major part of the *Kama Sutra* philosophy, making *Kama Sense Marketing* strongly different from Kevin Roberts's *LOVEMARKS*, which puts most of its emphasis on how to make the customer love the brand.

Jacob Levy

Marketing to Women

Modern gender marketing can find its origin in *The Ladies'
Paradise* by Émile Zola, published in 1883, in which the manager
of the new department store explains its unique gender strategy
toward women customers:

> "Yes," Mouret replied calmly, "in our shop, we
> like the customers.... That was how it really
> was; at the Paradise it was as if they were at a
> private party; when they were there, they felt
> constantly courted with flattery and showered
> with adoration, which entranced even the most
> virtuous. The shop's enormous success came from
> the seductive way it paid court to them." (325)

Like the suitors in the *Kama Sutra,* who want to bring pleasure
to the person whom they are courting and seducing, marketers
need to better understand their customers' emotional needs and
subsequently woo them using the art of love. To do so, we must
study the roles of men and women in the love and seduction
dance. We must research women's emotions, including attitudes
while shopping.

After moderating thousands of focus groups and conducting
thousands of surveys among women, I began to realize that we
misunderstand and underestimate women as customers. Their
decision-making process is unique and complicated, guided by
both rational and emotional elements that marketers cannot
fully understand. Their consumerism is more than just a means
of passing time; it is a language through which they convey their
stress and search for attention.

My observations suggest that as customers, women expect more
attention, flattery, reinforcement, sharing, and commitment. And
so it makes sense that women would also expect more love from

the products and brand names they buy and from the companies that supply them. With these observations in mind, I have devoted much discussion in this book to the subject of gender marketing.

After my first reading of the *Kama Sutra*, I tried to persuade some of my clients to adopt the emotional courting concept with their female customers. I asked one client, a marketing manager of a leading food chain, why he doesn't woo his female customers with targeted advertising or inside the store—especially given the fact that 66 percent of the customers entering his stores are women. Women arrive at his stores directly from work, exhausted from the stresses of their daily life, and yearning for a relaxed atmosphere and a kind word or gesture. My client quickly dismissed my suggestion, telling me he'd never considered it. Then he wondered aloud why he would give only female customers special treatment. Why not the male customers as well, in this era of mass marketing? On the surface, my client appeared to be making a good point. However, when it comes to marketing, men and women are not one and the same.

The woman's role in all buying decisions of the family is growing. In an effort to find out who is the main influencer in purchasing a household car, a series of in-depth interviews were conducted with male purchasers who had bought a car during the last thirty days. When asked directly who the primary decision maker was, one male answered boastfully, "Who else? It was me." Then the moderator asked him to describe exactly what happened.

"Well, one Sunday, I and my wife went to buy a car. I was planning to buy a Chevrolet sedan. As we walked into the showroom, my wife reminded me that our neighbors had bought vans, so when it was their turn to drive the Sunday school carpool, they could fit in all the kids. She had a point, and so I considered buying a van. But the showroom didn't have any vans we liked. So we tried the Ford showroom. One of them caught my eye, but when my wife tried it out, the steering wheel was too high for her. So we went from one van to another until we found one we both liked." And he continued: "When it came time to choose a color, I wanted a light color, but my wife wanted a dark one. So I said to myself, 'I won't be stubborn about this—at least let her choose the color.'"

Marketing strategies must define whether we are talking about male or female customers. While the concept of love presented in the *Kama Sutra* appears as a general and spiritual philosophy for both genders, the practical instructions in the ancient text refer to each gender separately. In most examples, the man appears as the wooer and the woman as the wooed.

It's All in the Table of Contents

The best way to share my excitement about the analogies between the *Kama Sutra* and love marketing is to bring the *Kama Sutra*'s table of contents together with its parallel analogies in *Kama Sense Marketing*. The ancient text is composed of seven chronological and logical parts describing the relationship between the men and women, all of which have their parallels in *Kama Sense Marketing*:

	Kama Sutra	*Kama Sense Marketing*
Part I	General Remarks	On the Philosophy of Love in Marketing
Part II	Amorous Advances	On Wooing your Customers
Part III	Acquiring a Wife	The Marriage Vow in Marketing
Part IV	Duties and Privileges of the Wife	On Maintaining Customers' Loyalty
Part V	Other Men's Wives	On Seducing Your Customers' Wives
Part VI	About Courtesans	On Choosing a Female Mentor
Part VII	Occult Practices	How to Tell Creative from Occult in Marketing

You've Got to Believe in Emotional Marketing

Three experiences in my professional (career) life have made me eligible for the Kama Sense Marketing journey: 1. my strong belief, still as a student, that purchasing and consumption are strongly affected by psychology and emotions. 2. my long life devotion to the marketing profession (as a multi-discipline of social sciences), and 3. my 40 years of experience as the founder and CEO of Gallup Israel, the first and largest marketing research institute in Israel. Where among other technologies, I was the first to introduce into Israel the concept of qualitative research and even have moderated hundreds of focused groups myself.

During my entire career I was an endless student of emotional marketing and as a consultant on the subject to scores of organizations.

The peak of my obsession with emotional marketing started some 30 years ago, at the early 80s of the previous century, when I became the consultant to the Dead Sea Health Products at Kibbutz Ein Gedi on the shores of the lowest lake in the world.

I was enthusiastically trying to convince the Kibbutz's management to believe that the Dead Sea minerals and black mud provide them with a huge opportunity to develop a new line of natural cosmetics based on ancient formulas. My excitement had magnified when I have realized that recent archeological excavations had discovered that at the first century AD the whole area was covered with cosmetic factories owned by Cleopatra herself.

It was only natural to suggest to name the new line as AHAVA, meaning in Hebrew LOVE . In addition to its strong emotional connotation, the new name lends itself to the Egyptian pyramids (the shape A which appears three times in the name), which symbolizes the ancient Egypt and Cleopatra its beautiful queen. Ahava products are successfully sold today all over the world.

In 1988 I have published my first book "The Writing on The Wall: The use of qualitative technique in political research in Israel." (Kivunim Publishing House).

After the sale of Gallup Israel to the American Gallup in 2001 I have co-founded together with my son Ori Levy the Trendum Ltd, the pioneer in the area of CGM (Consumer Generated Media) which dealt with automatic analysis of text over the Internet. The company was sold later successfully to Nielsen to become "Nielsen BuzzMetrics" the leader in this category.

Jacob Levy
Tel Aviv, Israel
April 2010

Acknowledgments

First and foremost, I would like to thank Vatsayayana the Hindu monk that some 1500 years ago, devoted his life to the collection of all there was to learn about the philosophy and practices of love—on which the ideas and knowledge of this book are based. Without him, the introduction of Love into modern marketing would have been considerably delayed. Should Vatsayayana be living today, I am sure he would become an excellent qualitative researcher (VP of emotional marketing).

And for the contemporary contributors, special thanks to Jessica Steinberg and Diane Sara Malka for helping me in both the editing and the translation of my ideas from Hebrew to proper English.

I am also greatly indebted to Tibor Weiss (US) my friend for 45 years, who injected into my examples his vast experience and creativity. Also bundle of thanks to a colleague and friend, Professor Aaron Shenhar from Rutgers University who had developed the revolutionary concept of SPL (Strategic Projects Leadership). Aaron has been trying persistently to convince me that introducing love into the organization thinking is a strategic project by itself. Also, many thanks to Miri Pritch and Nili Goldberg/Levy who have devoted of their precious time, and vast experience, for enlightening me on how love could be really introduced into modern marketing.

Jacob Levy

And finally, last but not least, to Gita, my dearest wife, and to my six children who had patiently endured my early 'crazy' analogies, until they were shaped in their final form.

Part One

On Philosophy of Love in Marketing

Chapter One

The Three Aims of Life

1. The Three Aims in Marketing Life

The *Kama Sutra*'s philosophy is based on the three aims of life, which appear in the beginning of the ancient book: Virtue (*Dharma*), Wealth (*Arta*), and Love (*Kama*), which *"must be pursued simultaneously, since they are connected to each other and are of the same nature" (16)*.

Kama Sense Marketing, as the ancient *Kama Sutra*, recommends that business organizations should also adopt the ancient three aims of life as a prerequisite for their success and as a basis for their long-term existence.

Artha and *Dharma*

The *Kama Sutra*, as a book on love, doesn't need to tell us how to accumulate *artha*, wealth, because it assumes that businesspeople know. For some reason, however, the ancient author felt he needed to allot some space to examples of the virtue statements, or *dharma* (27–28):

- Good deed, merit
- Law
- Underlying nature of beings
- Proper conduct
- Attaining future results by conduct required by the scriptures
- Invisible results of prescribed conduct
- Qualities of the individual
- Relative value of things
- Nonviolence
- Charity

Do you recognize some of the above statements in your organization's vision? If yes, to what extent does your organization really accomplish them?

Balancing *artha* with *dharma*. The idea of incorporating *dharma* into *artha*-based balance sheets, stock values, and mission statements is not new. Fortune 1000 companies already do so.

> Most high-profit organizations—especially the global ones—feel uncomfortable defining their business goals only in terms of *artha*/wealth.

In fact, whether due to their own convictions or outside pressures, most high-profit organizations—especially the global ones—feel uncomfortable defining their business goals only in terms of *artha* (profit, volume, or market share). They feel obliged to present *dharma*-based vision statements about making the world a better place. Indeed, it was encouraging to discover that, fifteen hundred years ago, the ancient *Kama Sutra* defined *dharma* as "that which supports the world" (28).

Balancing *artha* and *dharma* with *kama*. Very few companies include the term *passion* in their mission statements, and even fewer invoke the term *love,* as the notion of love in marketing is very new. Kama Sense Marketing states that *artha* and *dharma* should be balanced with *kama*. Doing so enables the organization to announce a super-mission statement, in which love is an important element. I call it super-mission for those who will place love as high as wealth and virtue in the mission statement and not make of it just another advertising gimmick at the end of the tactical plan.

Let's see how well-balanced the mission statements of Procter & Gamble, one of the world's largest global advertisers, are. P&G summarized its super-mission statement in three concepts: *Purpose, Values,* and *Principles.* Here are the specific mission statements[*]:

1. **Purpose:** "We will provide branded products and services of superior quality and value that improve the lives of the world's consumers. As a result, consumers will reward us with leadership sales, profits, and value creation, allowing our people, our shareholders, and the communities in which we live and work to prosper."

2. **Values:** leadership, ownership, integrity, passion for winning, and trust

3. **Principles** are explained in eight rather long sentences. (Respect for All Individuals, Inseparable Interests of the Company and the Individual, Strategically Focused, Innovation Is as a Cornerstone, the valuing of Personal Mastery, Seeking to Be the Best, and mutual Interdependency as a Way of Life)

In all three mission categories of P&G, spread on two pages, the term *love* doesn't appear even once. Time will come when there will be one additional category—*Love*—with a full explanation of how to achieve it.

---

[*]   As indicated in the PG web site on its mission

Here's how ignoring this third element of life—*kama*—can be costly:

Too much *artha*: After reviewing his highly profitable yearly balance sheet, Mr. Vardi, CEO of a large producer and importer of stationery products, invited a strategic consultant to help him draw up a new business mission statement. Mr. Vardi instructed the consultant to emphasize his organization's contribution to the environment with disposable stationery products.

When the consultant told him that research indicates that his consumers are not at all interested in knowing how disposable his products are, Mr. Vardi responded, "I make so much money, I feel obliged to do something for the community."

Mr. Vardi felt somewhat defensive and apologetic about his wealth and justified it by contributing to his community, thus balancing *artha* with *dharma*. Unknowingly, he was executing part of the *Kama Sutra* philosophy established fifteen hundred years ago.

But what of this third aim of life—*kama*? Should Mr. Vardi use *love* in his mission statement or behavior, could he avoid the need to promise benefits his clients don't really care about?

> **Should Mr. Vardi use love in either his mission statement or in his behavior, could he avoid the need to promise benefits his clients don't really care about?**

Based on the *Kama Sutra*'s three aims of life, we can tell Mr. Vardi: "Dear Mr. Vardi, you don't have to develop mission statements that your customers don't really care about. You would be better off investing in showing them in both your mission statements and your actions how much you really love them."

Defining Virtue and Love

There is no ground for virtuous behavior, since the benefits that might be obtained by it in the future are uncertain. (37)

When placing *dharma* and *kama* in their mission statements, organizations need to expand on exactly how they define virtue and what type of love they plan to adopt. They must distinguish between just a super-mission statement and the mission statement details.

Managers should be aware of the ancient warning against phony or insincere virtue statements that demonstrate the general notion that virtue statements are not made for fulfillment. When it comes to love and emotions, it becomes harder to deceive employees and customers, and you won't achieve your goals. Indeed, the ancient book insists: Do not write your mission statements if in the long run you do not intend to fulfill them. Otherwise you will never succeed.

Consistent, honest, and reciprocal. The organization interested in including *kama* in its mission statement should choose from a list of several types of love (see part 2). The most important rule to remember is, once you select a certain type of love, be honest and straightforward about it, and be reciprocal because in the final analysis, women cannot be deceived about emotions.

Marketers should understand that reciprocal love doesn't mean just a feeling of "being in love" on the part of either the customer or the marketers. It means an active love in which customers withdraw from their own budget to purchase the brand repeatedly while marketers endlessly create new ways to show their customers how much they really love them.

Love for the Community

*Vatsyayana considers that individual ethics, meaning the
accomplishing of one's individual social duty, are essential for success
in the domain of prosperity and love. (2)*

The *Kama Sutra* recognizes the very recent and modern buzz
of contributing to the community welfare, as long as the
contribution is honest and genuinely meant. Those who would
prove they really care about the community and show their care
not only in financial contributions but also in their inspiring
statements on virtue and love will better guarantee their success
in prosperity and love.

More on Reciprocal Love in Kama Sense Marketing

*Each of the two lovers must respond action with action; blow with
blow, for each activity the same activity, for each kiss a return kiss.*
(130)

True Reciprocity

The *Kama Sutra* insists on mutuality of relationship between two
people. Both parties must contribute equally to their relationship
in order to achieve true love. In Kama Sense Marketing, the
organization must truly love its customers in the same way that
it wants customers to love the company and its products. In this
kind of love relationship, the organization feels pleasure when a
customer is satisfied enough to buy a product again; the pleasure
is always mutual.

Some may argue that in marketing, unlike in romantic love,
emotional reciprocity is impossible since the customer pays
during the purchase and the marketer makes a profit. The ancient
text gives the solution to this paradox: *"It is generally admitted
that the man is active and the woman passive. The man's action is
therefore different than the woman's. The man thinks he is enjoying*

the woman, while the woman thinks that the man is enjoying her. There is thus a difference in attitude and experience, but not in enjoyment.... A difference in behavior does not imply a difference in results" (99).

Egoistical versus Self-Love

All love comes from egoistical desire. (211)

Unfortunately, not all organizations accept the reciprocity principle. They have an almost-egotistical interpretation of the meaning of love; that is, they would like their customers to love their brands. But they haven't given any thought as to how they can return or show love to their customers.

Erich Fromm, in his famous book, *The Art of Loving*, defined five types of love. One type is self-love, which, he explains, means that if an individual doesn't love himself, he will not be able to love his mate ("Love thy neighbor as thyself" or "The love for my own self is inseparably connected with the love for any other being" [Erich Fromm P 55]). Similarly, in Kama Sense Marketing, if the organization's staff members don't feel they are loved by the organization, they will not be able to love the organization and its brand. As a result, they will not be able to love their clients, and their clients, in turn, will not love their products. So love begins at home.

Proving mutuality. Kama Sense Marketing, just like the *Kama Sutra*, insists not only on the duality of relationships but also on an honest effort to prove reciprocity and mutuality. Customers who love a brand don't yet take for granted that the brand must show its love to them. When a brand does show its love, they are so excited and pleased that they go around telling everyone about it. It is still a novelty. However, while customers don't yet demand that the brand show its love, they may do so in the future, after competitive brands in the category start indicating how much they really love their clients.

Love for love. As students of marketing, we all accepted the concept that consumers expect to receive real value for their money. Modern marketers, as the P&G mission statement indicates, accept the concept of value for value. Kama Sense Marketing preaches adopting a completely new concept: love for love. If a company wants to be loved, it has to show love. Love goes both ways. It's a two-way street.

3. Love and Customer Support

Showing love to customers isn't just the task of the marketing staff. A company shows its love through the people who stand behind the brand: the sales staff, customer service employees, call centers—all the people who are in direct contact with the customers. These employees—whether on the phone or in person—can all prove their reciprocity in love.

Tide. Tide laundry detergent is considered one of the most popular detergents worldwide. In Israel, when a long-term loyal Tide customer has a question or a complaint about Tide and wants to talk to a Tide representative, she looks at the back of the bottle to find out whom to call. She discovers that Tide is manufactured by a company called Procter & Gamble, whose toll-free number is printed on the back of the container. She dials the number and, after waiting a while, she finally gets a person on the other end who says, "P&G brands, how can I help you?"

Our customer is sorely disappointed and, above all, confused. She expected to hear, "Hello, this is Tide. How can I help you?" Our customer would rather not discover that P&G also happens to produce Ariel detergent, a brand that she doesn't particularly like. She just wanted to talk to someone from Tide and instead, she's being sent through the corporate maze that is Procter & Gamble. She'll probably get the answer she's seeking after spending some time on the phone. But she'll get off the phone feeling disappointed and disillusioned.

She may still believe that Tide is the best detergent for her laundry, but the next time she goes to buy detergent, she may look at some other brands. Her sense of loyalty to Tide has been damaged. They didn't show her any love.

Tide, Ariel, and Persil are laundry detergent brands loved by millions. But are there human beings behind those brands? Think about it: It's fairly easy for a company to show love to its customers. Staffers at call centers and customer service departments can all be easily taught how to show love to the customers. In fast-moving consumer goods (FMCG), where store chains and not advertisers have the direct contact with the brand lovers, the advertisers should seize every opportunity to show their clients how much they really love them. P&G lost such an opportunity by avoiding the infinitesimally small cost of adding one more telephone number exclusively for Tide.

Woolite. The same holds for Woolite, a brand of Reckitt Benckiser—one of the largest European manufacturers of pharmaceutical and cleaning products. In Israel, if a Woolite customer would like to call the organization for a particular question, she will receive an automated answering service asking whether she is interested in pharmaceutics (dial 1), cleaning and esthetics (dial 2), Cologne's special deal (dial 3), and Cillit Bang (dial 4). The Woolite name is not mentioned at all—despite the fact that the call center phone number appears on the Woolite package.

4. Love in Your Marketing Strategy

Simply adding love to your super-mission statement is not enough. Love should be a part of your practical and actionable execution, a part of your marketing plan.

Love Must Be Planned and Controlled

Since eroticism is a universal natural phenomenon, common to all animals, certain authors ask why a treatise on eroticism is needed.
(33)

Vatsyayana argues with those who believe that eroticism is natural and universal and therefore shouldn't be planned or learned: "*The sages deem that virtue, interest, and pleasure must be coordinated: Given the importance of the preliminary acts, man and woman need rules of conduct*" (33).

Even in emotional matters, there must be planning and control. The *Kama Sutra* explains in great detail throughout the book that when dealing with emotions, both parties still employ planning and control, and it is planning and control that make human love different from that of animals.

Likewise, marketers must plan everything they do. Emotional messages must be part of an overall integrated campaign and not just the whim of a creative avant garde copywriter or ad agency art director. Companies must consider the mental processes necessary to form the emotional experiences that will ensure customer loyalty and commitment. For this, we need the *Kama Sutra*.

> Emotional messages must be part of an overall integrated campaign and not just the whim of a creative avant garde copywriter or ad agency art director

Not All Products Need or Support Emotional Marketing.

The need for an emotional experience stems from a deep and embedded consumer need for recognition, respect, flattery, and courtship.

1. Can the brand meet her emotional needs? It is not an axiom that all products must have emotional appeal: not all brands lend themselves to emotional/love marketing. It's the deep relationship between the consumer and the brand—or the culture and lifestyle surrounding the brand usage (and not merely the whim of the advertising people or the amount of money spent on it)—that dictates whether a particular brand can become emotional.

2. Can we tell when to trust our instincts? The *Kama Sutra* unveils the secrets of feminine behavior, telling us when to adhere to our instincts and when to be delicate or aggressive. Although some of us can use our instincts to help decide whether to adopt an emotional strategy, most of us need the *Kama Sutra*'s benchmarks, which can help open our eyes, expand our horizons, and provide us with a proper protocol for achieving our aims, as we will see in part 2, on wooing.

5. Love in Your Marketing Language or Lightning Flash Marketing

Unique channels. In one of its descriptions, the *Kama Sutra* suggests that love is a mysterious lightning flash that strikes two people. Once they are struck, a unique channel of communication opens up between the two. Suddenly, two people who are separate from one another begin to integrate, to understand, to communicate—even without words.

> **The potential consumer sees a brand and she knows this is her next purchase. She must have it.**

In the *Kama Sutra*, a boy and girl meet and there is already a language. The same thing happens between the brand and the customer. The potential consumer sees a brand, and she knows this is her next purchase. She must have it. She sees it and she says, "Bingo—that's what I want."

Love signals. In romantic love between man and woman, among youngsters, and even more among older people, the two parties don't have to talk to convey a message. They communicate quickly, based on a love signal: One wants to convey love, and the other wants to receive it.

Learning the shortcuts. Although many universities have separate departments that teach communications, there isn't a single school in the world that teaches how to communicate "in love" to women. We completely miss this issue. We use the same language to talk to our nonloving customers as to our loving customers. With the help of TV, Internet, and other electronic devices, we can now start to talk to our consumers with signs, shortcuts, and this language of love. We can more easily share messages and deepen relationships.

Intuitive processes. Based on the increasing numbers of marketing strategies using terms such as *relationship, emotional engagement,* and *service* or *buying experiences,* it seems that marketers are ready for these kinds of intuitive processes and relationships with their clients. They yearn for that lightning flash that will open the customer's eyes to the advantages of their products and secretly understand their communication, their language, and their messages. They hope for the stage in which the customer understands their smallest hints, which would eventually save the organization much effort and expense, including heavy advertising, repeated campaigns, and extraneous promotions.

Chapter Two

Kama Sense Knowledge
(Education and Research)

1. Need for a Knowledge Manager

*To succeed in the three aims of life, the first means is the acquisition
of knowledge. Without knowledge, almost any achievement is
impossible.(45)*

The above quote should be engraved on the walls of every modern business school around the world.

The ancient text urges every individual who wishes to improve his love life to conduct his own research before he puts any plan into action. In the introduction to the *Kama Sutra*, a whole section ("The Acquisition of Knowledge") is devoted to this subject.

Isn't about time to call marketing research the discipline of acquiring knowledge of all kinds, both qualitative and qualitative, from either internal (IT and databases) or external sources. The research institute department should be called the knowledge department and the director's business card should say: Manager of Knowledge Acquisition or Manager of Knowledge and Technology. Emphasizing the need for knowledge acquisition is not merely philosophical; it is a very practical consideration on which success or failure in the act of love hangs.

Vatsyayana's tenacity in promoting research throughout the book brings me to title him the world's first marketing researcher.

2. New Kinds of Research Are Needed

Based on insights and analogies of the *Kama Sutra*, we need two major areas of research and exploration. The first is aimed at improving our understanding of the consumer—the woman's emotional profile. This could be best described by the term *emotiongraphia*, somewhat similar to our current psychographics but with different stimuli and variables.

Emotiongraphia: More Than Demographics or Lifestyle

"If he does not perceive the woman's emotional state and, when he is burning with desire, begins his effusions without worrying about the woman's reaction, a man will always meet with failure…. Neither he nor the woman will experience true satisfaction" (111).

"He must reach the moment of action after studying the signs, contacts, and behavior of the woman from both physical and psychological points of view" (116).

Mood Research

A man should always be attentive to her mood before, during, and after the act. She should be treated like a flower.

The second area of research can be best described as *mood research,* aimed at measuring the consumer's emotions and feelings immediately before and during the act of buying. Part of mood research should be devoted to measuring reactions of the senses to different stimuli (discussed in part 2).

A woman can be moody on a particular shopping trip because of multitude of reasons, temporary and accidental; this is the domain of mood research. If she is constantly moody during most of her shopping trips, this is the domain of emotiongraphia.

In focusing only on demographics, and even only on emotiongraphia, market researchers neglect an area that undoubtedly affects women's behavior and purchases more than anything else out there: customer mood. That is, her mood while at the store—both before and during the purchase process—may affect her purchasing decision more than her age or lifestyle do. Some research suggests that more than 40 percent of all final buying decisions get made inside the store. Furthermore, research groups studying genders and markets have found that a woman's mood on a particular day or situation is affected by a host of factors—from different medications and vitamins that she takes to the season, her age, the day of her cycle, and other emotional factors—all unexplored by researchers.

By paying attention to the customer's body language, her way of talking, her questions and answers, or her reactions to stimuli presented by the salesperson, a sales professional versed in Kama Sense Marketing techniques can adopt his or her pitch accordingly.

Think of it this way: Everybody agrees that a woman who enters the store in an anxious mood should be treated differently than one who enters with excitement, affection, or boredom. The sales staff should be trained to recognize and accommodate those moods.

Feminine States of Mind

Since we still do not have a method for measuring mood, studying the effect of mood swings on a woman's purchasing behavior requires new tools and techniques. In research conducted recently among women shopping in a mall, respondents were asked to select from twenty-two words that best described their moods. Here are the results of thirteen positive words and phrases:

Moods of Women Shoppers

Pleasure	61%
Being pampered	58%
Feminine	42%
Excitement	21%
Temptation	19%
Sensual	15%
Relaxed	14%
Gentleness	12%
Affection	12%
Charm	11%
Desire	7%
Being courted	5%
Flirtation	5%

Interestingly, our list of 22 different moods—some of which scored high in our shopping survey—was copied from the *Kama Sutra*'s descriptions of a girl's mood before the act of love.

We should be aware of this mood issue. A woman's mood while shopping is expressed in the same words that describe her mood before the act of love.

On the Need to Relax Women

All is well if both are relaxed, like friends. But if not, how they will be reconciled (233)?

Stress, a natural part of women's moods, is a significant issue. In the above study, approximately one out of five women was under some kind of stress while shopping; that is, 18 percent of the women described themselves with at least one of the nine negative words and phrases (*anxiety, confusion, incapability, nervous, boredom, restless, worried, frustrated,* or *lost sense of self*).

In her book, *Just Ask A Woman*, Mary Lou Quinlan devotes a complete chapter to women's self-induced stress, in which she concludes: "To gain her as customer, first understand how to de-stress her life as a woman.... Like it or not, stress is standing between you and your marketing success with women" (30–31).

The *Kama Sutra* said the same thing fifteen hundred years earlier, accepting a woman's stress as a constant. Vatsyayana devotes a full chapter to the subject, "How to Relax the Girl," in which he says, "Although the girl has been obtained, she must not be utilized since she is still fearful.... Amorous games are necessary in order to relax the girl, without, however, deflowering her" (229–230).

In Kama Sense Marketing terms, marketers should never take the cash register rings for granted. They should constantly try to relax their customers in all phases of the relationship if they really want them to be valued, loyal, and loving customers. The *Kama Sutra* suggests many ways for achieving the wished-for relaxation: by giving gifts, by an appropriate conversation, or with the help of a female mentor.

Having thus pleased the girl with subjects suited to her mind and made himself agreeable, she becomes entirely relaxed. (236)

The final goal of all of those efforts is to win her trust, which is the basis for repeat purchases, loyalty, and advocacy of the brand.

When the girl is relaxed, she gives him signs of affection. (236)

Models without methodology. Marketing researchers are aware of the difficulties in studying emotions. It is a complex task. Experts resort to all sorts of techniques and sophisticated models for measuring customer emotions and, until now, they have been doing so without any accepted approach or methodology. Recently, some began experimenting with neurobiobehavioral models in marketing.

New emotional variables. We need a whole new list of emotional variables for segmenting women into meaningful emotional clusters. In today's marketing research, the closest we get to revealing emotional variables is via qualitative techniques (in-depth interviews, focus groups, and others), but their quantification remains unresolved due to subjective variable selection and subjective wording of the researcher's questions. We need methodologies that can utilize the best of both qualitative and quantitative analytical tools. That's exactly what the Observe and Converse methodologies permit us to do.

3. Observe and Converse Technologies

In several places, the *Kama Sutra* inspires very interesting new research approaches that should trigger the imagination of creative researchers: the methodologies of Observe and Converse. Although known for a long time to modern researchers and particularly to anthropologists, the suggested techniques should receive a modern twist—mostly in the quantifying stage.

Observe

He observes her reactions during religious ceremonies, wedding journeys, festivals, or when a funeral cortege is passing by, and it's by taking into account her state of mind at these different times that he manages to possess her. (255)

In romantic love, the attentive and mature man should always carefully observe his mate in an effort to study her needs, feelings, and behavior. It seems obvious, but so many men forget to do this—whether in our personal or in our professional lives.

In order to understand these states of mind, it is necessary to interpret the slightest signs.(113)

Anthropological observation. How does this work in the marketing world? Many marketing researchers borrow observation techniques from anthropology, commonly done in small groups or one on one. I remember reading in an Esomar magazine how P&G experts roam the world (especially in China), visiting young mothers in their homes and learning about their lifestyle and life habits in addition to how they change their babies' diapers. While in the past they were mostly observing the actual process of diaper change, now they try to understand the consumer's lifestyle and the place the brand holds in the customer's life before, during, and after actual product use.

In the absence of validated research models, marketers should constantly try to spend as much time as they can observing their loyal and heavy customers prior to, during, and after the actual use of their product, in real life situations. Which could undoubtedly bring them closer to their loved customers with more understanding and better decisions.

Body Language and Dress

This is why young men must know how to evaluate a woman's feelings from signs, her facial expressions, or the movements of her hands and feet.(250)

The question remains how to track, record, and analyze those observations for large populations. It won't be too long before market researchers, in synergy with programming and technology experts, will be able to measure basic emotions based on facial expressions, body gestures, dress color selected on the particular day, or any other techniques. There are already some new start-up companies that offer such technologies.

Converse

When they are alone, he says, "I have something to tell you." From her reply, "What is it about?" ... from her manner of closing the conversation, he can tell her state of mind. Her kind of reply is a test of her mood.... From those spontaneous signs he can tell up to what point she is in love. (254)

Conver-search. I was very happy to find out that the ancient *Kama Sutra* suggests what I have been pondering for quite some time: the need to use different questioning methods for women and for men. This makes a lot of sense in the marketing industry, which bases its questionnaire design on stimulus-response theories of behavioral research rather than on how women respond. Women need different stimuli. Since women can better reveal their feelings and behavior in open conversations, maybe the time has come to introduce "conversationnaires" rather than questionnaires. We can call the entire process "conver-search."

Back to Basics

To make her talk, he asks her questions in a few words, pretending not to know the answers. If he obtains no reply, without getting cross, he gently repeats his questions. If she continues to give no answer, he must not insist.... If one insists, the only reply will be shaking of the head. If one argues with her, she will not even nod her head. (232-3)

Let's expand on the role of conver-search, the emotional conversation between marketer and customer. Research should be brought back to where it used to be—without the formal questionnaires that are always a handicap and dependent upon depicting already-known variables. We want to return to open conversations in which one person expresses and the other listens, where people feel and hear with their ears and eyes, using their language spontaneously.

> *The woman's state of mind must be studied, her feeling examined.... He utilizes a messenger to ascertain her feelings prior to deciding. He must make use of an astute intermediary, who does not show preferences. (337)*

An "astute intermediary who does not show preferences" could provide a wonderful definition for the ideal objective and professional moderator we use today for qualitative research. So Vatsyayana prefers reading a woman's body language and listening carefully to her remarks and questions rather than resorting to the simple questioning techniques of current marketing research. Men will always have difficulties here unless they are well trained in advance, as the ancient *Kama Sutra* says on trying to understand the mysteries of women.

Men: closed questionnaires; women: open conversationnaires. The idea of using closed questionnaires for interviewing men and completely open conversationnaires for interviewing women shows that the methodologies suggested in the *Kama Sutra* are completely innovative, modern, and creative and prove deep knowledge and understanding of the delicate differences between men and women. It makes so much sense, and yet in my forty years of research experience, I have not come across many situations in which different research methodologies on the same topic were developed for men and women.

Conversation quantification. The question remains how to quantify complete conversations into meaningful analysis. Here, technology has made much more progress. For example, the automated text analysis models of Nielsen BuzzMetrics in the new category of consumer-generated media (CGM).

4. Gender Bias in Interviews

Asking questions, whether hearing or talking about embraces,
immediately excites sexual ardor in men. (111)

Neither the male nor the female interviewer can avoid introducing his or her own gender bias into the interviewing process. Let's say a research organization is interviewing women on their cosmetic experiences. If the interviewer is a male, each question could be loaded, even at the end, when the male might ask such a banal question as "How old are you?"

Furthermore, when a male interviewer meets a beautiful woman as his respondent, she may unintentionally affect his body language, his tone, and gestures. He will behave differently and his entire body language and his voice will change. By the same token, if a woman respondent is phoned by a male interviewer with a very sexy voice, she may give less accurate answers than she would to a female interviewer. For best results, men should interview men and women should interview women.

Logical to men, infatuated to women. To illustrate, we interviewed one thousand women to see where respondents stood on the emotional love ladder of *L'Oréal* brand. Half of the women were interviewed by male interviewers and half by female. As the table below shows, when women were interviewed by men, they tried to seem more cognitive and logical toward the brand by answering that they are in a stage of consideration of the brand, but when they were interviewed by women, they showed three times as much infatuated love for the brand.

Results of L'Oréal Love Ladder Study:

	Male Interviewers	Female Interviewers	Diff.
Infatuation	10%	30%	+20%
Passion	26%	23%	-3%
Confidence	18%	21%	+3%
Consideration	28%	11%	-17%
Affection	18%	15%	-3%

5. Emotional knowledge

If we are ready to accept the importance of the emotional relationship between companies and their customers, why shouldn't we extend our knowledge, understanding, and theories to the secrets hidden within the mysteries of love and courtship?

Unfortunately, business schools teach us very little about the opposite gender. One can find synergistic courses such as communication and marketing, marketing and psychology, or consumer behavior, but very little on the synergy between woman's emotions and her purchasing behavior. We must introduce love, emotion, and the art of observing women's behavior into the business school curriculum. We need courses such as: the arts of love in marketing, the emotional constitution of the woman (womanization) and its effects on shopping, the secrets behind the five senses, and how to research women's moods.

Studying the 64

How can the 64 arts be an object of worship? (209)

The 64 arts are an important part of the manual and practices of the *Kama Sutra* and, according to the ancient text, should be studied from childhood. "Vatsyayana includes the sixty-four arts, considered as accomplishments in the teaching of erotic techniques. Even in cases where it is not, possible to study them all, at least some of them should be practiced" (51).

Eloquence: from love life to marketing. Both men and women should also study the art of romantic love throughout their lives. They should do so openly and in formal classes. Courses in the *Kama Sutra*'s 64 arts of love will not only teach students how to improve their marketing skills, but they will also increase their general education—in addition to improving their love life and serving as an endless source of creativity. I strongly believe that those eloquent in the theory of love in their personal lives will have an easier time introducing love into their marketing practices.

Beginning at age ...? The 64 arts were taught to elementary school boys and girls in ancient India. While I am skeptical about the acceptance of the study of romantic love in today's elementary school curriculum, I think it's definitely possible to teach the 64 arts of romantic love in the behavioral sciences or marketing departments of our universities in order to induce creative use of those arts in modern marketing practices (see list of 64 arts of love in Appendix II).

Boys versus girls. According to the *Kama Sutra*, how we teach the 64 arts of love to girls differs from how we teach boys. While both genders should study the same 64 arts, which can prolong and improve love, women should study the arts of love only in their teens. As they mature, according to the *Kama Sutra*, women should avail themselves of more discreet, ladylike methods, learning from other women, such as their sisters, loyal nurses, favored aunts, and other female friends of the family.

If we accept the postfeminist concept that women are basically different from men when it comes to emotions, intuition, and instinct, then we will also accept that the study of marketing love should be different for each gender.

Premarital to Married

A woman should study even before reaching adolescence, and then, once married, should continue her studies with her husband. (48)

After marriage, women should continue studying with their husbands. This raises an interesting new learning possibility in marketing: Could marketers present the 64 arts of love to selected clients, in genuine learning sessions, trying to assess which could fit their particular brand (Flower bouquets, bed arrangements, table setting, art of playing drums, riddles, expert knowledge of stones and gems, massage and care of the body and hair, etc), provided they are related to the customer life style or her image of the particular brand, in which case both sides could equally learn how to obtain more information from the other "mate"?

Quality Control in Our Love Practices

Inevitably, there are mistakes in erotic practice that one must try to remedy. This law is valid at all times…. "defects must be eliminated" is the sages' point of view. (43)

In addition to advocating for extensive research, the *Kama Sutra* also promotes quality control to detect and correct defects, foul play, or just plain wrong behavior.

In management, one must always ask whether mistakes have been made and corrected. That's a basic tenet of quality control. The *Kama Sutra* says one can make mistakes in the way one treats one's partner, but take the time to think about it and next time the same mistake won't be made. This is the way we should all build our models for customer service. Don't ever take our partners—or customers—for granted.

Chapter Three

Women Marketers

Women Consultants

A master is one whose teachings lead to the achievements of virtue, success, and pleasure.

In the time of the *Kama Sutra*, those who wanted to learn about love went to the masters. With Kama Sense Marketing, a new kind of business consultant may emerge.

Although business executives currently use consultants, coaches, and mentors of all kinds, we also need experts on gender, emotions, and the use of the senses. Kama Sense consultants and mentors will help marketers to better understand female customers and how to use the 64 arts of love in their work. Specifically, I can envision the spread of emotional or love mentoresses to help male marketers succeed in their emotional marketing strategies. So Kama Sense Marketing must not neglect the concept of the modern female manager or mentor.

Natural Mentors

In addition to being the organization experts in charge of intuition and emotions, women are natural mentors and can coach men in their efforts to better understand women as customers or employees. Like Vatsyayana, I discuss this issue in part 6. However, I must add here a word of caution on the issue of the virile woman.

Women Managers Imitating Men

When the woman wants to make love like a man, it is called virile behavior. (182)

Kama Sense Marketing does not recommend imitating male managers. Vatsyayana does devote a full chapter to those women who take on the male role in the courtship and wooing process as a short-time game—but never as a long-time strategy. The following quote should be used as a milestone for virile women managers and consultants: "*Sometimes out of passion, custom, or temperament, the woman inverts the situation.... This is only temporary, however, and nature ends by taking back its due*" (164).

Women tougher on women. I've met many female executives in marketing: planners, marketing managers, brand managers, and account executives in advertising agencies. In most cases, these women reported to male bosses, and it was only natural that they adopt masculine behavior in order to succeed in their tasks.

Virile, or masculine, women managers will fail to attract the feminine customers, although they may very well attract male customers in the very few categories in which men are the sole decision makers.

Gail Evans, who has devoted much of her life's research to this issue, has written two books on the subject. In the first book, *Play Like a Man, Win Like a Woman*, she instructs women to imitate men in their business game. In her second book, *She Wins, You*

Win, however, she changes her mind. There, she recognizes this phenomenon in business organizations. She writes, "*Why do so many women often act much tougher toward the women who work for them than the men do*? (9). And then she recommends that women join forces inside the organization in order to create and prove their power. "*It's time ... for advancing as a group rather than as individuals*" (13).

Unique female strengths. This is still a defensive approach, one that underestimates the power of women. The increasing recognition of the importance of emotional perspectives in the business world—and particularly in marketing—opens a new and wide arena for female managers to show their particular and unique strengths as women.

Coaching Men and Women

Coaching the men. Although female managers may indeed eventually replace the men, rather than fighting to replace male colleagues, it will be easier for female managers to coach male colleagues on how to attract women customers and make those women love their organization and its brands.

Lifestyle mentors. Further, let female managers develop forums, communities, and boards of directors, through which women can exchange information about lifestyles and through which company brands can merge into their lifestyles. This new role opens a wide door through which women can increase their presence on boards of directors of Fortune 500 companies.

In a more emotional business world, women will have both the lead and the advantage. Women will be the "big sisters," the mentors to both male managers and female consumers. Modern research suggests that women use both sides of the brain while men use only one. In a more emotional marketplace, women can exercise their natural intuition and wider spectrum of both logical and emotional reasoning—as opposed to the decisive, one-sided approach often used by men.

The notion of emotional marketing opens a new path for women that will take them directly into top management positions and will change the balance of women on boards of directors in media, telecommunications, and e -companies, which currently stands at less than 9 percent, and of these women, only 3 percent had titles of C-level executives (CEO, COO, etc.), according to *Advertising Age.**

Women should therefore follow the steps of nature as specified in the *Kama Sutra*. They shouldn't fight against the natural advantage they possess in a world where emotions, intuition, and instincts are important. They should avoid following or imitating men's reliance on outdated rational and focused methods of thinking.

Women are today's world. In *Just Ask a Woman*, Mary Quinlan insists, "Before women call the shot on a decision, they rely on their personal board of directors, a cast of trusted advisors that women accumulate throughout their lives" (69). Quinlan is struggling to find a way to integrate women into today's world. Women are today's world.

> Quinlan is struggling... to integrate women into today's world. It's not a question for us: Women are today's world.

By adapting the *Kama Sutra* to our lives and society and by utilizing the thinking of ancient India, we don't have to struggle as much with figuring out how to configure women's role in society. It's much easier than we think.

Women fulfill three important roles: the major and most influential customers, the go-between or the matchmakers, and finally as coaches and mentors on emotional marketing.

---

* Advertising Age as quoted in "She means business" by Grant J. Schneider Tin Inc P15, P22

Action for the Introduction and Part One

1. Start by determining women's rate of influence on the household's purchasing decisions in your category. The man and the woman in the family should be asked separately. Use mostly quali-quanti techniques, since most men will be reluctant to admit their wives' impact on the final purchase.

2. Determine how important emotions are in the decision to buy and use products in your category. Establish to what extent your customers truly expect emotional benefits in addition to the physical and functional benefits they get from the different competing brands in your category.

3. Determine the degree of reciprocal love existing between your brand and its customers. For this, you need to measure:

1. The Brand Love Ladder, which measures the extent that customers love your brand (See part 2).

2. The Organization (Reciprocity) Love Ladder, which measures the extent that your customers feel that your organization really loves them in return.

4. Based on the above, decide on the type of love you wish to establish with your clients. (See part 2.)

5. Regularly survey your employees to determine employee feelings toward your organization and products. More specifically:

1. Do your employees love their place of work and its products?

2. Do your employees feel the organization loves them in return?

6. Add LOVE to your super-mission statement. Establish your super-mission *kama* statement and integrate it into your general corporate mission promise. Frequently test to what extent employees, suppliers, and clients know of your super-mission statements. Customers do not object to your profits if you show them your love. They may even respect and honor organizations that make profits.

7. Change your research philosophy into quali-quanti techniques of Observe and Converse with your loved ones (your customers). Until technology is developed for analyzing conversations and observations on large samples, *train a cadre of ethnographers and experts* in the semiotics of your particular product category. One-on-one is preferable. Conversationnaires, specialized conversation techniques with women conducted by female interviewers, are preferable to the normal closed questionnaires.

8. Be aware of your customers' stress. Although we do not yet have methodologies for identifying and measuring a woman's mood while entering the store, bear in mind that many of your women visitors may enter your store under stress. You can put yourself one step ahead by being aware of this and creating the right sensory environment (detailed in part 2). Very experienced and sensitive sales clerks could contribute much to this endeavor.

Part Two

On Wooing Your Customers

The Love Mix Theory and Its Activation through Personal Marketing

What has been said up to now concerning sexual relations has been said briefly, being intended for intelligent men. We will now explain in greater detail for people who are hard of understanding.
(102)

I'm not insulted by Vatsyayana's sarcastic comment. If the practicalities of love are only for the slow-witted or hard of understanding, then I'm proud to be one. "Amorous Advances," part 2 of the *Kama Sutra*, is its longest chapter, since the wooing process is essential to reaching true love. Having explained the philosophy of Kama Sense Marketing in part 1, the rest of *Kama Sense Marketing* is devoted to the practical question of how to ensure love in marketing.

Chapter One

The Love Mix Theory
Harmony between Preludes and Conclusions

Marketing Mix Theory

Like all marketing students, I was raised on the Marketing Mix theory, a concept developed by Neil H. Borden in the 1950s. The theory claims that an ideal marketing strategy is achieved only with an ideal mix between the "Four Ps":

Product (product development and brand management);

Price (accounting and pricing);

Promotion (advertising and PR); and

Place (distribution and merchandising).

The Four Ps, throughout my entire professional life, have always provided me with a structure for my marketing thinking and planning. However, once confronted with emotional marketing, I realized the shortcomings of the Marketing Mix theory: at least three of the four Ps are over once the brand is on the shelf.

Love Mix Theory

We need a new mix theory that accounts for what happens after the product has reached the shelf. I call this the Love Mix theory. The Love Mix theory starts where the Marketing Mix ends, as most of the active wooing process—both the Preludes and the Conclusions—

> The active wooing process (the Love Mix) begins once the product has reached the store. From then on, the wooing never ends.

begin after the product has reached the shelf. From then on, the wooing never ends.

1. An Ideal Love Mix Is When Preludes and Conclusions are Considered Together

The preludes and conclusions form part of the act of love. (202)

The first and most important rule of wooing, in both sexual and marketing relationships, is that lovemaking is a continuing process that should never end, because the road to a woman's heart is long. In Kama Sense Marketing, the wooing process begins with the first advertisement for the product, continues through the first contact

> Lovemaking is a continuing process that should never end, because the road to a woman's heart is long.

with the product in the store, and ends—or never ends—long after the actual experience of using the brand or product.

Single Peak, Multiple Peaks

When he has ejected his semen, he seeks rest, whereas she wishes to continue. (98)

During the first purchase, the marketer, the wooer, experiences only one peak—the ring of the cash register. On the other side of the counter, the woman customer experiences multiple peaks: the actual experience inside the store, the purchase, the actual experience with the product, and, later, the reinforcement she receives from her partner or friends.

So when the woman achieves orgasm—or makes the purchase— she will continue to experience and expect pleasure. Marketers will do well to remember that.

Just as the before and after in lovemaking are as important as the act itself, marketers must likewise heed the need for both foreplay and after play. Currently, marketers exhibit several levels of awareness on this issue.

First-purchase marketers. Most marketers rely on advertising hints ("teasers") to lure customers into taking the product off the store shelf and over to the cash register. They hope the product's first use will persuade the consumer to buy it again. Most major cosmetic manufacturers fall into this category. At each "new launch," they place most of their marketing efforts into advertising or point-of-purchase (POP) at the counters.

Repeat-purchase marketers. More sophisticated marketers understand they must work harder to bring customers to the second, third, and future purchases.

Emotional-branding marketers. A few experts truly grasp that the real challenge lies not only in motivating the repeat purchase, but in winning the customer's heart and soul. They may spend time and money studying emotional branding to better understand their customers; they may create emotional, sensual, and provocative advertising. But they don't tell or even show their female customer that the company

> **The real challenge lies not only in motivating the repeat purchase, but in winning the customer's heart and soul.**

loves her from the very first contact and is doing everything to please her.

Kama Sense Marketers. Kama Sense Marketers begin their advances amorously, since the customer—a woman, in our case—is not always ripe for lovemaking. The female customer should be constantly wooed and courted to propel her toward buying the product and later becoming loyal to that product.

> They don't tell or even show their female customer that the company loves her from the very first contact and is doing everything to please her.

Preludes and Conclusions: Part of the Wooing

The signs of affection must be continued before and after the sexual act.(197)

Preludes—The Foreplay Before and While Buying

In order to seduce a woman, it is necessary to know erotic technique... To achieve one's ends, preliminaries are indispensable. (89)

Just as a successful sexual union requires "preliminaries," as foreplay was termed back in the *Kama Sutra* era, so do marketing and selling. The preludes mostly refer to activating the Sensory Mix—the appropriate mix of senses for that product.

Conclusions—The After Play.

The woman's desire does not calm down after she has been satisfied.... A man's excitement ceases once he has ejaculated. A woman's need is not satisfied at that point, since woman's nature is not like a man's. (95)

Women customers need after play in their experience with the brand. In fact, the customer shouldn't be left alone with the product. Once the customer has purchased the product, she needs more instructions, explanations, and reinforcement for using the product (or for buying it again). It is just at that moment that she expects to be courted—to be reminded of the product and its benefits and of the belief and trust in the company's love and affection for her.

Role of the marketer. The first role of marketers is to make the customer so happy with the brand and the organization that she becomes a loyal and committed client, an advocate who recommends it to others. A second role of marketers is to remind the consumer of the brand experience when the need (direct or indirect) arises.

> The first role of marketers is to make the customer so happy with the brand... that she becomes a loyal and committed client, an advocate who recommends it to others.

2. Preludes Begin with the Multisensory Concept

The preludes to the act are essential; they involve touching, smelling, speaking, and looking. (210)

In most cases, marketers restrict themselves to using two senses— sound and sight—and use them mostly in advertising, neglecting the other possible senses and venues within the Sensory Mix. Sure, there is the Procter & Gamble bus-stop billboard that allows pedestrians to press a button and smell the Head & Shoulders scent or the Samsung campaign to spray specially selected scents in their flagship store in Manhattan. But these have become textbook examples because they are so rare.

The More Sensory, the Better

In marketing brands, as in loving people, the more sensory the encounter with the brand, the stronger the emotional experience with the product and the more secure the belief in the product.

The five senses of wine drinking. Consider, for example, why wine drinkers are so passionate about their wine experiences. First and foremost, because the wine-drinking experience involves all five senses. It starts with *sight*, when the drinker appreciates the shape and label of the bottle. It continues with *touch*, when the buyer caresses the bottle, trying to sense its temperature and moving on to the rituals of opening the bottle. Then comes the *sound* of the cork when it leaves its nest. Next, the experience is all about *smell*. The wine drinker sniffs the cork and then pours the wine into a glass, sniffing the contents for its flavors and aroma. And again, the sense of *sight*, when examining the color and texture of the wine in the glass. And then again, the sound of clanking crystal, which reinforces the emotional feeling of togetherness. Finally, after the other four senses have been fully satisfied, the drinker gets to *taste* the wine, which is the ultimate satisfaction in the wine-drinking experience.

> People drink wine with all of their senses. It's an act of love, just like the actual act of love in which all five senses are also deployed.

People drink wine with all of their senses. It's an act of love, just like the actual act of love, in which all five senses are also deployed, a fact that is emphasized throughout the *Kama Sutra*.

Women respond. Women are much more responsive to the five senses than are men. Research shows that women have a sharper sense of smell, sound, and even taste than men. Their innate capacity to employ both sides of the brain—the cognitive and the emotional—together with their unique hormonal structure and its effect on the brain centers makes them more sensitive and more sensual than men, who mainly rely on the left, cognitive side of the brain. A consumer who uses both sides of the brain provides more faculties to market to—an ideal receptivity to be activated by the creative marketer.

Marketers often forget that what they're selling is atmosphere and not merely a product. Think of it this way: If a customer enters a store as a result of being triggered by sensory advertising and doesn't see or sense a continuation of those sensory prompts (for example, when the store atmosphere is a complete contradiction to what the advertising conveys), she may be disappointed and leave, and the advertiser could lose a potential customer.

> [Women's] innate capacity to employ both sides of the brain—the cognitive and the emotional—together with their unique hormonal structure and its effect on the brain centers—make them more sensitive and more sensual...[providing] an ideal receptivity to...the creative marketer.

It is very common to see a sexy print or television campaign for clothing, showing a couple in a provocative situation. When the woman who is triggered by this campaign is tempted to visit the advertised store, in some cases she may not see nor feel any of the atmosphere triggers suggested by the ad. She may enter into a poorly lit facility, with clumsily dressed sales clerks, with messy store shelves and disorganized, and with background music that is not conducive to the mood she would have anticipated.

Buying the pub experience. A variety of senses is engaged at the Abercrombie and Fitch store on Fifth Avenue in Manhattan. Visitors are greeted at the entrance by a young, handsome man, naked from the waist up. He directs shoppers entering into a full pub atmosphere: dark, sensually illuminated, with loud pub music and couches to sit on and enjoy the scene. Young people feel this is where they want to be; this is why they buy. I could hardly find my way in the dark through the dense crowd and wondered how anybody could see what he or she was purchasing. Yet, at the exit, they were all holding filled bags.

3. Engage in Six-Sense Marketing

Kama is the enjoyment of appropriate objects by the five senses of hearing, seeing, tasting, and smelling assisted by the mind together with the soul.... The ingredient in this is a peculiar contact between the organ of sense and its object, and the consciousness of pleasure which arises from the contact is called Kama.

—*The* Kama Sutra *of Vatsyayana, Richard Burton and F. F. Arbuthnot (77)*

The above quote provides one of the best definitions of marketing ever made, by suggesting that "the mind together with the soul" constitutes a sense by itself—that is, the sixth sense.

Marketing: art more than science. The *Kama Sutra's* definition would view marketing as the art—rather than the science—of activating the senses. Even the good old Marketing Mix, initiated more than half a century ago, compared a successful mix to the art of cooking. In this case, the chef mixes together all sorts of ingredients—some existing and some completely new—together into a tasty dish, which for practicality and accountability is called the marketing plan.

Marketing is an art based on a multitude of emotions, instincts, and intuitions orchestrated together by the soul but eventually written down and tracked for accountability by the mind. More so for the Love Mix, which brings together the senses into an emotional harmony by practitioners of many creative disciplines—product designers, store experts, advertising experts, sensory experts, and more—all based on intuition or the soul.

In order to succeed, these five senses have to be mixed in an ideal harmony, which will differ from product to product, or from lover to lover. This harmony is the soul, and it is put together by intuition. The intuition and instincts—messengers of the soul—bring together the instruments and create the music.

Somebody has to write the music for each instrument and must put them together into a plan. And this is when the "mind together with the soul" comes into play. The mind plans the music and evaluates: "This is possible and this is impossible," "The piece has to be three minutes," and so on. This is a cognitive process analogous to the marketing plan. Indeed, this is where the soul and the mind come together.

Then, despite the fact that the music is written down, the conductor has to reproduce the soul message of the composer and conduct the music so that people will hear it in a way that the composer wanted it to be heard. In this analogy, the conductor fulfills the same role as the marketing manager.

Intuition and marketing decisions. By adding the concept of the soul and mind as a sixth sense, Vatsyayana unveils one of the secrets of marketing success—it gives further legitimization to the role of intuition as a major factor in the marketing plan.

> **One of the secrets of marketing success—*intuition* as a major factor in the Marketing Plan.**

This creates a new distinction between selling, product design, store arrangement, and advertising (which depends mostly on instinct, intuition, and creativity) and marketing (which puts it all together with the help of the mind-soul into one multidisciplinary harmony).

> **Selling is instinctive and intuitive...while maerketing is planned...The mind plans from the soul's creation.**

Selling is instinctive and intuitive (an emotional process), while marketing is planned (a mental process). So the mind plans from the soul's creation.

Intuition and sensory capture. Purchasing is also instinctive and intuitive: the instinct of the female consumer captures the marketer's sensory signals, causing her to form an initial bond with the brand, which is the basis for drawing her emotional attention.

So in order to attract and influence the consumer, we must consider the sensual elements of the product and its design—touching, seeing (the package, the label, the content), smelling, tasting, and, in some cases, hearing. We must also consider sensual elements of the marketing and selling environment (what goes outside the product)—in the store, on the shelf, and in advertising.

4. Inspire Your Sensory Mix with the 64 Arts

Each of the 64 arts can be easily adapted to modern marketing. The 64 arts of love (listed in appendix II) provide endless ideas to inspire a creative marketer in implementing an appropriate Sensory Mix. Consider two examples from the long list: "tattooing" and " making beds":

Art of tattooing. The first page of Martin Lindstrom's *BRAND Sense* tells of a young boy, Wilhelm Andreas Petrus Boise, who appears at a doctor's office, asking the doctor to remove a Gucci tattoo that he'd had inked into his neck five years earlier. "Gucci had become more than a brand. It was my one and only religion," said the young Wilhelm. "The admiration I had for the Gucci brand was stronger than for any other person I knew. For me, Gucci was more than a brand—it was my personal companion." Lindstrom then presents survey results on which brand people would be willing to tattoo onto their arms: Harley-Davidson was first, with 19 percent, followed by Disney, with 15 percent, and Coca-Cola, 8 percent.

It was very refreshing to read on the beginning of 2010 that the Chanel's Spring 2010 collection, to be sold at Selfridges starting March 1, includes temporary tattoos, which feature the iconic double C's, lace, rosary beads, Karl Lagerfeld's beloved chains, and some **Cinderella**-worthy birdies.

Art of making beds. Wouldn't it make sense to ask each new hotel guest to specify, via an interactive TV screen, what kind of pillow arrangement she prefers or whether she requires an extra blanket or has any special requests for bathroom toiletries? A former Israeli tourism minister once told me the

> It's so easy to make people happy, to act on the small gestures that show you really care.

following story: Some time ago, he had registered at a five-star hotel in Copenhagen. He loved the service and the hotel during his visit. About five years later, when visiting Copenhagen again, he decided to stay at the same hotel. The registration clerk recognized him, by his name, as a former guest and offered him the same room he had had five years earlier, which happened to be vacant at the time. But the best part of the surprise was when he found an additional pillow on his bed with this note: "During your last stay with us you requested a very fluffy pillow, so we thought that you would like the same kind of pillow again."

It's so easy to make people happy, to act on the small gestures that show you really care. What is important to recognize about the 64 arts is how they appeal to the five senses and, ultimately, to the sixth sense, the soul—that all-encompassing part of us that has to be won in the wooing process. Creative Kama Sense

> The 64 arts...appeal to the fives senses and, ultimately, to the...soul—that all-encompassing part of us that has to be won in the wooing process.

marketers can choose any of the 64 arts of love to appeal to each of the consumers' five senses and win their love, trust, and loyalty.

64 =2⁵. In my opinion, mathematics can give the mystical number of 64 another twist; 64 is 2 to the power of 5, which means that the ideal Sensory Mix is when the two mates employ the five senses to the utmost.

5. Build Your Unique Sensory Star

Kama: **Eros with Planning.** Although some marketers and consultants have already begun to recommend employing the five senses, Vatsyayana's real innovation lies in never using those five senses without proper planning. *Kama* is Eros with planning, he says, and this planning is what distinguishes humans from animals and what permits the analogy between the *Kama Sutra* and Kama Sense Marketing.

> Vatsyayana's real innovation lies in never using those five senses without proper planning. Kama (love) is Eros with planning.

So we have six senses: sight, smell, touch, hearing, tasting, and mind/soul. In the marketing industry, the concept of using all six senses is still not fully appreciated by most companies. Marketers have neglected the five senses and especially the sixth one, in both designing products and creating the sensory environment needed to sell those products.

> Marketers have neglected these six senses both in designing products and creating the sensory environment needed to sell those products.

Sensory Star. Think of the Sensory Mix as a five-sided sensory star. Although the length of each point depends on how much that sense adds to the product and the selling situation, all five senses are represented, with the soul at its center.

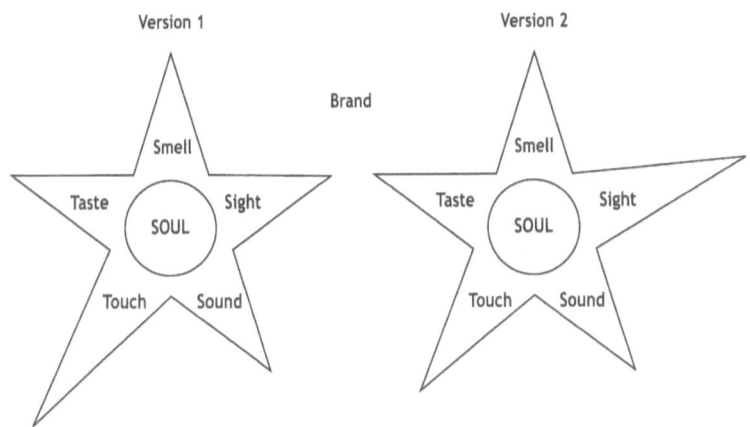

The Sensory Mix Formula

Sensory (Kama) Product

What goes into the product (including product and package design)

+

Sensory (Kama) Environment

What goes outside the product (advertising, promotion, and in-store distribution or in call centers)

=

Kama Sense Marketing Success

The ideal Sensory Mix, where the marketers can achieve their emotional goals (love)

Organizations will achieve their goals only if they resort to emotional marketing. Organizations are late to utilize the six senses because they simply don't give proper attention to emotion and love.

Of course, this requires truly learning the arts of love. It's never a good idea to feign and boast about one's knowledge of the arts of love. Women customers will recognize and scorn any company that doesn't bear that knowledge. Without actual learning, marketers and

> **This whole book… hinges on the assumption that organizations will achieve their goals only if they resort to emotional marketing (love).**

companies will never reach a long-lasting and true love with their clients.

If marketers follow that advice, it won't be long before the following ad will be a regular feature in most Help Wanted sections:

Wanted: Marketing Manager versed in the arts of love.

6. Things to Consider When Planning Your Sensory Star

When planning your sensory star you should take into consideration the time of day and the attraction practice your brand enjoys.

Timing the Sensory Mix

The use of the five senses in Kama Sense Marketing should be spread throughout the entire relationship with the customer, from its initiation in advertising or at the point of purchase to the actual experiences with the product and the repeat purchase.

The consumer's senses can be activated at three major points: In advertising, at the point of purchase, and while the customer is actually using the product. The first two are under the direct control of the marketers and so are easier to watch over and manipulate. The third, the point of product use, is outside marketers' reach and is therefore full of question marks. We could define those three activation points as the PPP:

- place (of interaction),
- product (physical characteristics), and
- point of time.

Time-of-day messages. Time of day, often neglected, could become a critical issue. A woman will respond to radio or billboard advertising differently when stuck in morning traffic than at night at a mall, bar, or restaurant. Since most billboards can be electronic or two-sided, drivers should see an advertisement for coffee in the morning and for beer or wine in the afternoon and evening. Instead, most advertisers today tend to hit their customers with the same message regardless of where they are or what their mood.

In amorous practices, the man's behavior should take into account the place, the country, and the moment.(167)

Traveling, cheering. At the 1996 Atlanta Olympics, Coca-Cola used different messages at different points of interaction with the customer. At the airport, their billboards said, "Traveling is thirsty work," while at the games, on buses, and on the city streets, the billboards read, "Cheering is thirsty work."

Time-of-day sensory cues. Time-of-day advertising takes on even more meaning when introducing senses into the mix. During the evening, stores could activate different kinds of music, lighting, or scents than during the morning.

Preludes Should Rely on Previous Attraction Practices

Those who know the mechanics of relations say that attraction is born in four ways: from practice, from imagination, from substitution, or from the object.(103-105

Creating an attraction among customers requires some kind of emotional interaction with the brand. The ancient *Kama Sutra* lists four ways for drawing such emotional attraction; the same four apply beautifully to the marketing environment.

Attraction from Practice

All activities of the senses, starting with speech, require continuous "Practice" … to manifest themselves. Love is born of long practice, like the love of hunting for the hunter.(103)

In Kama Sense Marketing, attraction through practice is when a woman buys a product she has tried before or knows of through a friend or sister. It is the past experience that facilitates brand extensions, when a producer approaches his long-standing customers with a newer version of the brands already recognized and cherished.

Palmolive family. Take dishwashing liquid, as an example. Palmolive is a well-known and beloved brand, so good that Marge used it to soften her hands in the famous 1970s commercial. When Palmolive extends its family of dishwasher detergents with a new brand, it expects a certain degree of commitment from its existing loyal customers, thereby saving advertising and marketing costs.

Marketers should find a way to give those special customers the impression that the organization is tuned to its customers' needs and is bringing them an additional version of the brand they know and appreciate so much.

Attraction from Imagination

A person with no previous experience of a form of action can develop an attraction born of "imagination" … One may desire something without having any experience of the act…. Imaginary love, which is a kind of affective condition, is termed pure mental invention.(104)

Broken-record versus conventional advertising. In most cases, any attention paid to a brand is at first "imaginary"; that is, the woman develops an imaginary love for a brand she has never seen or tried before. The development of an imaginary love is the domain of advertising and public-relations creativity. Some would argue that word-of-mouth advertising is much more effective and efficient than any conventional advertising in developing love for a brand-new, unrecognized product. But there are certain dangers in relying on word-of-mouth advertising—mainly, the so-called broken message.

The broken message is similar to the end result of the childhood game Telephone, in which everyone sits in a circle, and one participant whispers a message into the ear of the person sitting to the right. That person whispers what she understood to the person next to her, and so on, until the message comes back to the initiator. The initiator tells the group what word she received and what word she started with. It's a funny game, but the ultimate distortion proves that additional advertising is usually needed, even when the decision is made to rely on word-of-mouth.

Emotion-activating imaginative advertising. There is a great need for advertising that activates emotions through imagination, as it can create emotional expectations even before the brand is tried. Furthermore, in many cases, and especially in durable goods, the brand's emotional image may be developed after its first purchase, magnifying imaginary advertising's effectiveness.

Attraction through Substitution

> *In the absence of someone, one becomes attached to another ...*
> *called "substitute" attachment.... When a man or a woman can*
> *mentally transfer their feelings to another person, attributing to the*
> *new object the qualities of the other. (104)*

Attraction through substitution is when someone uses one product instead of another from the same category. A very good example is the whole area of private labels sold by the large chains: Consumers buy the private label for a reduced price, assuring themselves it is produced by a large and famous branded manufacturer.

Too Early Bird. Substitution plagued a nature-based cosmetics manufacturer that once created an introductory advertising campaign for a new line of products several weeks before the new product line actually reached the shelves. Customers influenced by the advertising campaign walked into drugstores asking for the product, were disappointed to find that it hadn't yet been stocked in the stores, and were persuaded by the salespeople to buy a competing brand.

Attraction from the Object

Whether manifested openly or implicitly, love based on the desire for material goods, in which gain is primordial, is of another nature.
(105)

Attraction born of the desire for the object, the material good, is a mercenary love, in which the customer buys the product because of gifts or prizes. Sales promotion plays a major role here; for example, two for the price of one, or a large discount for those buying during the "next three days." This attraction is somewhat dangerous, because it does not lead to loyalty and love.

Accepting the match. All of the above methodologies are legitimate as long as both sides, the customer and the marketer, accept the match. For example, if marketers decide to attract customers by the object (price) approach, they must make sure that the price is right and that the customer knows it. This is not the case with other incentives. For example, in creating an imagery love, sometimes it may be wiser or more appropriate to increase the price, activating the "price = quality" phenomenon.

7. The Senses in Detail

On Sight

In sexual life, sight is a weapon of primary importance.(211)

Looks and beauty are important to both wooer and wooed, and sight is undoubtedly the most developed sense in marketing. In the ancient *Kama Sutra*, most of the 64 arts of love deal with sight, and sight is recognized by the *Kama Sutra* as the most seductive sense.

Spending millions. Organizations spend millions on the design and look of logos, packaging, and products. This is where advertising and product design experts utilize most of their creativity. Indeed, advertising agencies have long recognized and exploited sight, often disproportionately. Beyond that, an entirely new discipline, visual merchandising, has been invented to activate a customer's emotions when she enters the store or approaches the sales counter—using aisle placement, POP signs, and the like. Marketers are constantly increasing their budgets to explore the possibilities of visual merchandising, a subject taught at almost all the schools of design and communication.

But do POP and visual merchandising take full advantage of all the possible triggers that the 64 arts of love offer us with the use of sight? For example, when a line of salted crackers is extended into additional flavors such as barbecue or pizza, has enough been done to reinforce the barbecue atmosphere (showing a family smiling around a barbecue grill, for example)? Has enough been done to consider the possible impact of packaging on the use or user of the product? If the original Coca-Cola was designed to insinuate a unique sensual shape, why can't the same be done with other products?

When a man sees, even from afar, nail marks on the girl's breasts, he feels interest and desire for her even without knowing her. (137)

Using sight to arouse interest. Can marketing be more provocative with the skillful use of sight? The *Kama Sutra* suggests that even the slightest visual hint of the sexual act can almost always arouse potential partners, offering a preview of the delights to come.

> **Even the slightest visual hint of the sexual act can, almost always, arouse potential partners**

Proof of a purchase can arouse the interest of other customers in many ways. Consider store shopping bags, an area of design that has taken off in the last decade. Whenever a salesperson identifies a loyal customer, whether by recognition or via a symbol on her computer screen, she can give her a special bag showing everybody that this woman is a preferred customer of said store.

Using sight to pamper. Airlines know how to do that very effectively with their platinum customers. They pamper them in luxurious business lounges that activate the senses of taste and touch. The interior design of the business lounge, with its comfortable couches, is very relaxing and reinforcing to the anxious traveler and adds to the fantasy of the food served there. The airlines are showing their frequent flyers how much they love them.

There are other methods of using the sense of sight to pamper and help customers. When a woman shops for a dress for an evening party and she enters the store during the day, the fitting rooms and store lights can be properly dimmed to convey how she will look during evening hours. Three-sided mirrors in the fitting rooms can allow women to see how the dress looks on them from different angles.

From visual to sensual. With Kama Sense Marketing, it may be more appropriate to shift from visual merchandising to sensual merchandising, in which students learn how to activate as many of the senses as possible, each with varying strength.

In some brands, the smell may be relatively stronger and more important, but for others, the label or the container may be more important.

On Smell

Each man and woman has a smell of his or her own. There is a connection between body odors and sexual excitation.(210)

Secret Scents. Diana Gerard walks into the Victoria's Secret store on 57th Street in Manhattan. She is in a seductive mood but doesn't know exactly what she wants to buy. The overall plan is to surprise her husband, John, and create an evening of pleasure for them. They will be celebrating their twenty-fifth anniversary tonight. Her senses are sharpened, and she feels her sensuality increasing the moment she enters the store. Memories of previous purchases at this store are wafting over her, making her pleasantly excited about what could await her this time.

Victoria's Secret is one of Diana's favorite stores. She loves its dim lighting and spacious aisles. She loves the soft classical music that surrounds the shopping experience. She thinks to herself that the Mozart quintet currently playing is one of John's favorites, which introduces his virtual presence into the store. She is particularly moved by the sensual and suggestive scent emerging from the aisle and wonders whether this exotic smell is sprayed intentionally by the store management or is the perfume of the attractive woman who just passed in front of her.

Every step she takes into the store brings a sense of relief, as if Diana is shedding another layer of the worries and stresses of the day. Her walking pace becomes slower; her face is calmer, with a small, discreet smile developing on her face. She is ready to be wooed and seduced by the store, unconsciously waiting for a saleswoman to offer assistance and to find just the thing that will match her mood this afternoon. She will accept help from any of the saleswomen because she is ready to be pampered, and she knows that's what she'll get from Victoria's Secret.

After half an hour of trying on different lingerie, she selects the one most seductive and flattering on her. The saleswoman gives her the impression—discreetly—that she had made the right choice. While the saleswoman is wrapping up her purchase, Diana thanks her, saying, "I love shopping here. I always find something I like."

Effect on lovers. Smell, which has a strong effect on lovers, plays an essential role in the Marketing Mix. Smell is increasingly recognized for its effect on moods of customers, and particularly of women, who have a more developed sense of smell than men do.

Unresearched, underutilized. The sense of smell, which was strongly influential in Diana's purchase, is the least researched and least utilized sense in marketing. "Less than 3 percent of the Fortune 1000 list have even given it a thought," claims Lindstrom in *BRAND sense.*

Remembered for generations. It's true. Most marketing manuals referring to using the senses mention car manufacturers that develop special scents to keep a new car smelling fresh until the car is sold. One hotel chain created a scent sprayed throughout its public spaces to relax and invigorate the guests. And the Samsung Experience store at Manhattan's Columbus Circle experimented with spraying Calvin Klein One on the escalator and at the entrance to the store to attract shoppers.

Yet these examples are few and anecdotal. It's a shame because smell and scent are such an elementary experience, vital in creating an emotional atmosphere and environment. Scent ignites unique nerve centers. Many experts agree that people can remember the impact of a certain smell for as long as fifty years. Crayola has trademarked the smell of its crayons because their scent is remembered for generations. Even with food, the aroma of certain dishes can often play a more important role than the actual taste of the food.

Scents: symbols of love. Marketers need to think creatively and ask themselves where there is cause for adding a scent to every marketing and advertising campaign. They should think about adding smell not only to enhance the product sensorially but also because adding scents is a symbol of love for their clientele. Real estate agents spray baking smells in kitchens to help sell properties. Major supermarkets spray fresh baking odors at the store entrance to activate the customer's taste buds. Wouldn't it be nice and effective if fashion stores would spray different scents at different times of the day?

Scented logos. From now on, marketers will need to consider adding scents to their logo. The dictionary suggests that a logo is mainly visual. Why shouldn't marketers add additional unique sensory cues? If Singapore Airlines can add its own unique scent to its planes, why can't other corporations add unique scents to their lobbies, elevators, and waiting rooms?

Strawberry jam billboard. I was once in Paris to attend SIAL, a large food exhibition in Paris. As I crossed the street, I smelled strawberries, a spring fruit that I love. The smell reminded me that I hadn't had any breakfast, and I immediately felt like having a croissant with strawberry jam. I looked around for the source of the strawberry scent and, to my disappointment, I saw that it was coming from a billboard advertising strawberry jam by one of the exhibitors. The scent didn't get me any strawberries, but I'll never forget what it was advertising. I forgave the brand for arousing my appetite in vain; the advertising for the visitors to the exhibition had been effective. If there had been strawberry jam in the vicinity, I would have bought it. The smell aroused my senses.

Jacob Levy

On Sound

It is a matter of experience that music reaches the center of female sexuality.(211)

In today's world, it seems that marketers forget or neglect the influence of sound on female customers and on their moods during the different seasons or times of day. Sound is used primarily in television or radio advertising. However, the use of voice and sound in other aspects of the purchasing process is still virgin territory for marketers and researchers.

Distinctive Sounds

The sound of music, jokes, interesting stories all create a certain physical excitement.(211)

Sound of the car door. It is not only the sound of music. Do marketers properly utilize sound to strengthen the emotional relationship with their clients? Some do. Nokia and its immediately recognizable opening ringtone and the Microsoft music when starting the Windows program both come to mind. The speed of the melody's appearance gives users the confidence and knowledge that their black box is ready to perform its daily miracles. Carmaker Daimler-Chrysler established a research and development unit at the end of the 1990s charged with developing an attractive sound when their car doors closed.

Background Music and Purchasing

Music is connected with the science of sound, which is one of the basic elements in understanding the creation of the world. (48)

Bad rap. I can think of many instances when I've walked into a café in the evening, looking for quiet respite, only to find loud rap music playing in the background. And it's not just cafés. Clothing stores worldwide fall prey to this problem; one wonders if the storeowners have ever explored the impact of the music they play.

"When I walk into a clothing store or any other store where the music is too loud and edgy, I will most likely leave the store without even recognizing why," said Danna Salth, from an interview conducted in-store to measure the effect of music on the buying process for one of my clients.

Muzak, the global maker of public background music, began conducting research in the 1930s on using music to improve workers' productivity and influence consumers' shopping habits. "Background music is a kind of aural pheromone, attracting some customers and repelling others," wrote David Owen about Muzak ("The Soundtrack of Your Life," *The New Yorker*, April 10, 2006). By playing customized Muzak in their stores, companies—primarily retailers—were creating retail theatre, said one former Muzak executive. "I realized then that Muzak's business wasn't really about selling music. It was about selling emotion—about finding the soundtrack that would make this store or that restaurant feel like something, rather than being just an intellectual proposition."

Men's Voices and Purchasing

Women find an emotional attraction in the sound of their lover's voice. Women can be hypnotized by a man's voice and be attracted by him. This is why Vatsyayana attributes great importance to hearing. Singing and music are incitements to love.(211)

If a man's voice works such wonders, has enough been learned about this effect in order to teach salespeople how to talk and—when needed—how to listen to female customers?

Provocative Sounds and Purchasing. Why not offer more creative and provocative situations for using sound and building triggers in the marketing process? If spas use Eastern and Indian music to elicit relaxation and meditation, why not use different erotic sounds and music for creating attention or excitement during the buying process?

The *Kama Sutra* detected seven different sounds during the sexual act (160):

1. Himkara—nasal "hee" starting from the throat and mounting to the nostril and breaking out as a light sound

2. Stanita—"ha" from deep in the throat to the nose, like the rolling of thunder

3. Rudita—weeping, a clear sound that should be moving

4. Sutkrita—sighing by drawing in the breath, "sou-sou"

5. Dutkrita—cry or pain.

6. Kujita—slow "kou-kou"

7. Photkrita—violent expulsion of pain

A stereo manufacturer could use some of those erotic sounds to draw attention to the benefits of a bedroom stereo system. If those seven unique sounds—recognizable to nearly everyone— were used in a provocative commercial, there's no question that people would be drawn to seeing what's being advertised.

If Sally could do it with Harry, why not take it a step further?

On Taste

Products that are pleasant to lick are made of powdered aphrodisiacs mixed with honey, which may be sweet, salty, sour, or bitter according to the choice, which are chosen at the right moment to reinvigorate the body or stimulate amorous ardor.(p 53)

Aphrodisiac food. The *Kama Sutra* knew all about the effect of food, flavor, and tastes on lovers' behavior, but in our day, very little research has been done on the effect of different ingredients on the behavior of male and female eaters and their mood. Cocktail parties are planned for the purpose of achieving certain corporate goals, and yet nobody thinks of preparing the appropriate foods that will elicit certain reactions, responses, or conversations. Such consideration may be seen in the privacy of a romantic anniversary or Valentine's Day dinner or in celebrating someone's birthday, but what about a broader view? It's time to think about how companies can create foods that will arouse the customers' senses and their sense of loyalty to the product.

On the surface, the contribution of taste to the sensory star appears to be simple. Most taste research tries to establish how different flavors affect taste buds and which flavor is preferred for the largest consumer base. Under those circumstances, there is very little to add regarding the importance of taste when selecting a winning food brand. However, it's not really that simple. People eat with their eyes and with their nose before they ever even let the food touch their mouth. The colors and scents of the food strongly affect one's perception of how it will taste.

All taste buds. In general, women are more sensitive to taste than men are. They actually have more taste buds than men do.[*]

And younger customers are more sensitive than older customers. Do all food manufacturers take those factors into account? On which age groups are they conducting their research, and to which are they directing their products?

Most taste buds are spread around the mouth, mostly on the tongue. That's why wine drinkers tend to move wine around in their mouths in order to give all taste buds a chance to try the wine. But that's just wine. How can the taste process of other products be further perfected?

---

[*]   http//Library.thinkquest.org/3750/taste/taste html

The *Kama Sutra* complicates the issue even further by suggesting that "Food is of four kinds: bitten, eaten, licked, or drunk," adding new dimensions to our sensual marketing or our sensory star.

Would it be possible to instruct customers, when applicable, to use two or more of those eating modes in order to further enjoy and savor the taste of the company's brand? Could a brand name encourage customers to start with licking the product and then moving to biting and eating it? Why not recommend keeping the food longer in the mouth or shifting it around inside the mouth, not only for increasing taste sensations, but also for better digestion and weight control.

Multitaste modes. A good example of a brand that has utilized at least three of the four tasting modes is the Australian Tim Tam, a chocolate-covered cookie that's very popular among the Aussies. A fad developed that was called the Tim Tam Slam, which spread from Australia to other countries that sell Tim Tams.

Wikipedia defines the Tim Tam Slam as, "the practice of drinking a beverage by sucking it through a Tim Tam, an Australian chocolate-covered biscuit, with both ends bitten off." According to the *Toxic Custard Guide to Australia* (Tim Tam – Wikipedia), this procedure is done as follows:

1. Prepare a cup of tea (or another hot or cold drink).
2. Remove the Tim Tam from the packet.
3. Bite a small section off two diagonally opposite corners.
4. Dip one corner into the drink.
5. Suck on the other corner, which will mix the drink with little pieces of the biscuit.
6. When the Tim Tam begins to fall apart in your hand, eat the whole biscuit.
7. Obtain another Tim Tam from the packet and return to step 3.

Anthropological research based on observations made inside consumers' homes revealed completely new insights on how customers use and eat different kinds of foods. People who spread their cottage cheese on bread or crackers with a little jam have completely different impressions and requests about cottage cheese texture than those who eat their cottage cheese with a spoon directly from the container or with their salad or melon. Can one brand be extended into two sub-brands, one for spreading on bread or crackers and one for eating with a spoon?

It's true that from time to time, the marketer needs to change or add something to a product in order to meet the customer's needs and lifestyle. Manufacturers need to start classifying their customers according to the way they use different brands in the category. There are those who drink Coca-Cola straight from the bottle, those who prefer a glass bottle to a can, or a can to a plastic bottle, while still others like their Coke in a glass with a slice of lemon but don't want to drink Diet Coke with the lemon already added. Are they all different in terms of their emotional bond with Coca-Cola? Is it possible that their emotional experience is different?

On Touch

A whirl of pleasurable sensations is connected with the perception of the organ of touch. (29)

Intimacy and Ease of Touch

In the act of love, from beginning to end, touching predominates. (210)

Touch as an intimate sense. Touch and taste are the two senses closest to the body and therefore more intimate than the other senses, which are external to body. As such, they have limited use in advertising, being applicable only (1) at point of purchase and

(2) during product use. It should be a real marketing challenge to explore these intimate senses.

Ease of touch. Most customers want to feel the product. Some marketers create fantastic products and packages that draw the consumer to touch and feel the product. But are those packages part of a sensual or sense-driven strategy? In other words, does the packaging allow the customer to feel the product?

For example, women like to feel the fabric when buying lingerie or pantyhose. In most stores, different brands of stockings are hung on the sides of each rack, allowing buyers to feel the product and assess the knit, silkiness, and weight of each kind of pantyhose. Same with nightgowns, bras, even most underwear. But what about those closed underwear boxes? It's much harder to decide to buy panties enclosed in a box that doesn't allow the shopper to touch and feel that most intimate of garments. The same principle applies to almost any limited-access product that people buy on a regular basis.

Tissue testing. In my neighborhood supermarket, a toilet paper manufacturer hung up an open roll, inviting customers to feel its softness. I stood there for ten minutes and noticed that almost everyone who tested the toilet paper put a package of it into their shopping cart.

Design and Touch

Product design: the touch that sells. Consider Crocs, the light-as-a-feather, brightly hued, plastic cloglike marketing marvels. Introduced as a slip-resistant deck shoe by a Colorado company, they have become the all-purpose shoe for people of all ages. A series of small nubbins on the shoe's sole makes them the comfort shoe of choice for people who are on their feet all day and for fashionistas who love the bright hues. Bottom line—they're comfortable, and the feel of them is what makes them so popular. To touch and wear Crocs is to love them.

Package design: Touch this package! Knowing what an important role touch plays in life, the sense of touch needs to be introduced more into packaging. If caressing a wine bottle and wine glass are so elemental to creating a multisensory atmosphere, why not introduce those sensations to other products, such as olive oil? Olive oil producers have not yet fully explored the opportunities that lay within the shape and feel of their bottles and corks, the green tones denoting its quality, its smooth taste, or the entire Sensory Star that is part of the ritual of pouring olive oil and creating a meal.

POP design: Touch this product! The Sephora cosmetics chain allows its customers to try every product in the store, making products more familiar and convenient for the customers. It's much easier to buy blush or eyeliner if the customer has actually tried it on and can see how it looks and feels on her skin.

Certain Body Shop stores have sinks so that customers can wet a loofah or sponge and try out the company's bath products.

Wineries that invite customers to visit the winery, try their products, or hear lectures on wine tasting are spending their money well, as indicated by the constant rise in worldwide wine consumption.

Touch Substitutes

Touch can't always be worked into the initial contact and experience with a product. But companies that can't let their customers touch their products, such as service providers, can show their love for their women customers by offering them touch-based body treatments, spa visits, or massages as a token of appreciation and attention.

Touch Strategies

Most touch strategies should be directed toward actual use of the product. Cereal manufacturers love when children enter the kitchen and eat cereal by themselves. But have they studied the difficulties of a small child trying to pour milk from a heavy container? A touch strategy must include milk containers specially built for children.

Touch-based vacation memories. Years ago, I visited Hayman Island in Australia, where I had a superb vacation at a great hotel, situated on one of the most beautiful beaches in the world. While staying there, I bought a long plastic shoehorn at the hotel shop. Ten years later, I still use the shoehorn whenever I have to struggle with a stubborn shoe. Each time I touch it, I notice the hotel logo, which immediately brings a smile to my face. The shoehorn cost no more than twenty-five cents to produce. It is amazing how many pleasant memories and associations a hotel can gain for just twenty-five cents.

Touching is part of life; it draws one person to another in a way that no other sense can. It's the same for products: to touch something is to know it a little better. It's the personal touch.

8. The Conclusions: The BUYER Theory

In order to emphasize that buying is only the beginning and not the end of a relationship with the client, I have developed the BUYER Theory. This theory introduces a fixed mode for planning, research, and actual execution—indicating how long the wooing process could extend after the actual purchase:

B= Buy
U=Use
Y=Yield
E=Experience
R=Reinforce

This challenge suggests that the initial purchase contact with customers is not enough, nor is it the means to the end. Rather, it emphasizes the need to continue and track the relationship with the customer long after the actual purchase if we really want to assure repeat purchase, loyalty, and love. The more marketers understand how customers—particularly women—experience the purchasing process and the potential enjoyment from that progression, the better the chances of their marketing and selling success. The BUYER Theory has research, marketing, and relationship implications:

Buy. The store is the site of half of all switching between brands and over two-thirds of buying decisions. Do we really recognize the decision-making process and the customer's mood while she is inside the store planning to buy a product? Is the mood of a woman trying to buy a refill for her makeup the same as the one trying to buy something new for her evening date? It is indeed a challenge that opens new research horizons for future understanding.

And how about the after purchase?

After making love, one's behavior should be affectionate. A solid attachment is established through friendly conversation. (201)

Use. Do we really know which of the family members use the brand, how they use it, and whether they know how to utilize its benefits? Is our product design (content and convenience) satisfactory to all family users?

Yield. Do we know to which functional and physical benefits the customer is attentive?

Experience. Do we know what kind of emotional experiences the consumer gets from using this particular brand?

Reinforce. Do we understand the importance and process of the reinforcement a woman gets from her girlfriends or mate? Are there ways the marketer can help the customer converse and convey her experiences with her peers? Such conversations are essential both for developing brand loyalty and for recommending to others.

After-the-Sale Loyalty Teasers. The BUYER concept is important not only to track emotional experiences with the brand after or while in use—which eventually will improve the emotional relationship with the client—but also to help the marketer develop a new kind of marketing teaser to activate the sequence.

Contrary to selling teasers, which draw the consumer's attention before the actual sale, loyalty teasers draw the user's attention after the sale, while using the product, or even afterward. Loyalty teasers capture the client in her home and encourage her to use the brand more frequently. It is a reinforcement teaser. Consider one challenge: Could Tetley find a way to influence its customers who are constantly undecided about whether to drink coffee or tea to prefer tea, which will automatically increase Tetley tea consumption?

In all my research experience, I've had very few cases in which the marketers asked me to conduct research solely for describing:

1. how and when each family member uses the brand,
2. how and when the customer decided to select a particular brand in the pantry, and
3. how the customer felt when using said brand.

These three research topics undoubtedly require dedicated research planned purposely for unveiling the BUYER elements—a research protocol that does not yet exist in its entirety.

9. The Love Mix Puts It All Together with a Soul

It is worth a reminder of the importance of the sixth sense—the soul, together with the mind—in putting the Preludes (Sensory Mix) and the Conclusions (BUYER theory) into one strategy—

the Love Mix Strategy—like the maestro who conducts the orchestra in generating the necessary harmony of love.

THE LOVE MIX

Preludes		*Conclusions*
Sight		*Buy*
Smell	←*Soul*→	*Use*
Sound	←*Mind*→	*Yield*
Taste		*Experience*
Touch		*Reinforce*

Chapter Two

Personal Marketing
A New Kind of Segmentation

1. Love Mix Must be Personal

Activating the Love Mix strategy requires a personal approach to the consumer. According to Kama Sense Marketing, each customer has to be courted and wooed individually, on a personal basis, as if she is the only customer.

One Person at a Time

"The best way to build a brand is one person at a time," said Howard Shultz, Starbucks founder, in *Pour Your Heart into It: How Starbucks Built a Company One Cup at a Time.* Modern marketers sometimes fail to realize that behind the masses in mass marketing are customers, individuals with individual needs, such as Suzy, Rachel, and Diane. This is what the peer approach is all about: finding and maintaining the focus—and the love—of each and every customer.

Give impression it's made especially for her. Kama Sense Marketing calls for a new practice—giving the customer the impression that the product is especially made for her, in addition to the marketer's efforts to reach her, woo her personally, and develop a personal relationship. Kama Sense Marketing calls for new types of questions to discover:

- How can the marketer reach the right loving consumer?
- How can he woo her personally?
- How can he give her the impression that the brand or the service centers are made especially for her?
- Do we really know how she uses the product at home?
- How can the marketers develop a personal relationship?

It is not direct marketing. The direct marketing people (defined as BTL, below the line) will say it's very simple. The pantheon of BTL is full of successes and fascinating stories, and the growing penetration of the Internet is making it even easier to identify and pursue individual clients. But most of the current direct-marketing practices deal with how to reach and sell mass-produced products to individuals. Personal marketing gives each customer special emotional attention, for example, by using web and mobile technologies for recognizing the customer, her behavior, and her real functional and emotional needs when she enters the store rather than when she approaches the cash register.

So Kama Sense Marketing is interested in the above-the-line (ATL) strategy, with conventional advertising and retail distribution, but using modern technologies to approach the courted clients, giving the feeling of personal marketing. It is necessary to think about how—in an era of mass marketing and globalization—each customer can be courted and wooed on an individual and personal basis. In other words, we need to consider how to segment each customer on a more personal level. To this end, Kama Sense Marketing provides the necessary variables for a new kind of segmentation, "Peer Segmentation."

2. Peer Segmentation Is the Solution

The best relationships are with people of the same religions, who have the same values. If they are different, it is more difficult ... to have a good relationship. (223)

With the help of the web and mobile technologies, Kama Sense Marketing's niche approach can inspire many new ways of thoroughly and sensitively segmenting customers effectively and efficiently. These kinds of amorous advances can't be executed in groups. Each customer must be given the feeling that she is the one and only customer.

When the married couple has the same pleasures, tastes, and amusements, they enhance each other's value. This kind of marriage is recommended. (224)

Segmentation by needs and emotions. Most current conventional segmentations are either based on demographics (teenagers, Baby Boomers, African-Americans, twentysomethings, etc.) or on lifestyle and psychometrics (the innovators, the health seekers, etc.). Both techniques are unsatisfactory. Demographic segmentation does not necessarily explain differences in emotional constitution or in consumption, and lifestyle segments are good to know but ultimately hard to reach or activate. Yes, it is very interesting that one's product is also used by the trendsetters. But how and where on earth can those trendsetters be found and, let's be honest, exploited?

Reachable small groups with similar needs. Segmentation must identify small groups with similar needs who can actually be reached. With peer segmentation, the common denominator will be mainly emotional needs and variables. Using modern technology, marketers can identify smaller, more specific groups of customers, almost down to the individual and personal level, as long as the customers in each peer group have a similar cultural

77

background and emotional lifestyle and are looking for a similar courting process.

3. Emotional and Gender-Directed Segmentation

Accordingly, the *Kama Sutra* offers a multitude of segmentation criteria, which may fit rather larger groups of women while still granting each the feeling that she is the only one.

To answer the needs of the individual customer in mass, or ATL, marketing, we need a very sophisticated classification system that is both effective and efficient—a customer classification system much smarter, and even more daring, than ever known before.

Kama Sense Marketing offers three segmentation criteria from the ancient text: age classification (a new approach), size of organ (physical energy), and type of love chosen.

Age Classification

The *Kama Sutra* places special significance on age, with each age and stage of life deserving and receiving a different courting process (116):

> Adolescent (*bala*): sixteen years old
> Young woman (*taruni*): sixteen to thirty
> Mature woman (*prudha*): thirty one to fifty
> Old woman (*Buddha*): over fifty

Deep understanding of modern needs. This classification, although somewhat simplified, provides a deep understanding of both the physical and psychological needs of modern women. A young woman of thirty loves to think of herself in the same category as someone who is sixteen, while a girl of sixteen is always trying to convince herself and her peers that she is as mature as a woman of thirty. With the advancement of medical knowledge, gender medicine, and life expectancy, we can slightly update those classifications for today's world. (Conventional research generally classifies respondents as 15–24, 25–34, 35–44, 45–54, 55–64, and so on.) Accordingly, a woman between the ages of thirty and fifty would be termed a "real woman," and the over-fifty woman, a "mature woman." The fifty- to sixty-year-old women would be defined as "experienced," and the over-sixty-five as "senior" women.

50+. Consider, for example, the physical and mental needs of the mature woman that warrant special attention. This age can bring hot flashes, osteoporosis, different dietary and digestive needs, hormonal deficiencies, and depression. Some companies, particularly in industries such as cosmetics, have begun to realize the importance of this age group and are already directing special products and advertising campaigns to the 50+ category. Maybe the time has arrived for assigning special divisions or category managers for each of the age groups.

30+. There are also specific needs and products for the 30+ group. A *New York Times* article by Adam Sternbergh ("Up with Group," March 26, 2006) describes a new generation group:

> It is a story about 40-year-old men and women who look, talk, act, and dress like people who are 22 years old. It's not about a fad but about a phenomenon that looks to be permanent. It's about the hedge-fund guy in Park Slope with the chunky square glasses, brown rock T-shirt, slight paunch, expensive jeans, Puma sneakers, and shoulder-slung messenger bag, with two kids squirming over his lap like itchy chimps at the Tea Lounge on Sunday morning. It's about the mom in the low-slung Sevens and ankle boots and vaguely Berlin-art-scene blouse with the $800 stroller and the TV-screen-size Olsen-twins sunglasses perched on her head walking through Bryant Park listening to Death Cab for Cutie on her Nano.

"When I was a child, I spoke as a child, I understood as a child, I thought as a child: But when I became a man, I put away childish things." This cohort is not interested in putting away childish things. They are a generation or two of affluent, urban adults who are now happily sailing through their thirties and forties, and even fifties, clad in beat-up sneakers and cashmere hoodies, content that they can enjoy all the good parts of being a grown-up (a real paycheck, a family, the warm touch of cashmere) with none of the bad parts (Dockers, management seminars, indentured servitude at the local Gymboree). It's about a brave new world whose citizens are radically rethinking what it means to be a grown-up and whether being a grown-up still requires, you know, actually growing up.

Mature-age wooing. Some industries, such as banks, cater to their well-to-do clientele with special divisions, creating private banking or the platinum club through which management woos its customers and their well-padded bank accounts. But food manufacturers haven't considered doing the same for their mature customers.

For those products whose purchase is affected by age, food manufacturers could be organized internally according to the ages of their female customers. A manager of the 50+ division, for example, could sell the company's products and services to those women more effectively, rather than being a one-brand manager for all age groups. Such divisions could adopt feminine names—Diana, Suzy, or Lisa, names appropriate for the different age groups—and each department would develop different courting techniques according to the age and needs of their potential customers. Take, for example, Marks & Spencer's previously mentioned campaign featuring 60s model Twiggy for the 50+ crowd*. (Marks&Spencer's sales increase fuelled by Twiggy ad campaign by Julia Pearlman Brand Republic 11-Oct-05)

Adeg Aktiv Markt 50+. During the last two years, the Austrian supermarket chain *Adeg* launched a series of new stores in Salzburg and Vienna specially geared toward their senior customers, under the name Adeg Aktiv Markt 50+. In order to accommodate their senior clientele, Adeg incorporated everything from reduced-glare lighting and slip-proof flooring to wider aisles and easier-to-navigate parking spaces. Reduced-height shelving, pleasant places to sit, and signage and shelf markers in larger type are part of the reorganization as well. Stores also offer several cart and basket options, including a shopping cart that attaches to a wheelchair and another with a fold-down seat for shoppers who might want to rest along the way. The produce display is engineered so that even a person in a motorized cart or wheelchair can select his or her own items. Shoppers can borrow reading glasses to check small print on labels or use magnifying glasses attached to shelves in some areas. Smaller packages of items such as cheese are intended to serve households of one or two. Notably, all employees are over fifty.

If it works in Austria, it can work anywhere. The point is, different customers—whether of varying ages, sex, or lifestyle—have different needs. And marketers need to answer those needs.

Size Does Count (Physical Energy)

According to the size of his sexual organ, a man is called a hare (shasha), bull (vrisha), or stallion (ashva). The woman, according to type, is called doe (mrigi), mare (vadava) or cow-elephant (hastini). (89)

Given the *Kama Sutra*'s focus on sex, it's not surprising that classification according to organ size is heavily emphasized throughout the *Kama Sutra*. But, men, take note: Size differences are not for men only. Moreover, size doesn't matter if the user knows how to handle and maneuver the size he—or she—possesses.

In Kama Sense Marketing, the size-of-organ analogy opens many new creative avenues in marketing and has three important implications.

The mutuality (reciprocity) syndrome. The old adage that "size does matter" is brought to a different level. Size *does* matter, but since both men and women face the same categorization, it's not just the customer's problem. The customer's "size"—or whatever physical problem she experiences in health, body measurement, et cetera—is the marketer's problem as well: The marketer has to compensate for that problem, because no one's perfect.

> Manufacturers should make sure to compensate for whatever problems and needs the customers may have.

Unmatched sizes are the general rule. The three masculine sizes crossed over the three feminine sizes form a nine-cell matrix, where only three cells (diagonal) have a perfect match and another six (the majority) do not match. This means that a perfect match is the exception. Since in most cases matching is not ideal, both parties have to struggle for successful match. Manufacturers should study and understand the needs of their customers and cater to those needs as personally as possible, making sure to compensate for whatever problems and needs the customers may have.

It is temperament that adjusts it for all. It is because of temperament that some women wear dress sizes that do not perfectly fit them. In Kama Sense Marketing, marketers should learn how to convert physical handicaps into marketing opportunities.

> The customer's "size"—or whatever physical problem she experiences—is the marketer's problem as well… because no one's perfect.

This classification does not merely refer to the physical aspect, but also implies a certain kind of temperament.(90)

The *Kama Sutra* suggests that those with unmatched sizes may solve the problem with their temperament. In Kama Sutra Marketing terms, this means that the customer wants to buy the brand as much as the marketer wishes to sell it, in order to consummate an emotional interaction, and that both the escorted girl, as well as the wooer, should do everything to address those physical deficiencies.

In Kama Sense Marketing terms, this means that consumers may have a variety of physical handicaps that the marketer should address and compensate. Both marketers and their female customers need to compromise and come up with creative means for handling requests and needs that at first may appear impossible—but that is what marketing is all about! It's about loving the customers, despite any problems they may have. The physical incompatibilities and special needs of female customers present marketers with tremendous opportunities.

Type of Love Segmentation

After the classifications according to age and physical needs, the moment arrives to deal with the emotional factor. The *Kama Sutra* recognizes different kinds of love: Some are deeper and more sensual, and others, more superficial. There is young love and old love. But most important, the partners must agree to, or at least acknowledge, the type of love they intend to engage in with one another. The *Kama Sutra* describes six types of legitimate love, listed below; following each type are quotes from clients' in-depth interviews illustrating Kama Sense Marketing terms:

- Passionate love: born of physical attraction (love at first sight). "I don't know why, but I feel I must have this product."

- Love born of habit: the result of affection produced by long cohabitation (a simple but true affection but without true erotic attraction; love born of consummation). "I bought the new Clinique lotion because, for the last ten years, I have been using only Clinique!"

- Feigned love: without true feelings (false desire, occasional sex). "I keep on buying the brand during the special offers, get all the benefits, and move to another promotion with another brand. This advertiser gives me the feeling that this is exactly how he wants me to behave."

- Substitute love: love acts are taken over by the interposition of another party (a man sleeps with his wife while thinking about another woman). "I buy the chain's private label because I am convinced they buy it from a leading manufacturer, so why should I pay more for a famous brand?"

- Degrading love: to satiate one's basest instincts (a form of sexual release like neutral sex for money without love). "I buy only fake watches. It gives me the feeling of being trendy every couple of years."

For the purposes of Kama Sense Marketing, the above six types of love are analogous to relationships with customers. Not all love relationships with customers must be passionate, love-at-first-sight conflagrations.

The company-customer relationship, while significant, could also be defined as habitual love, substitution love, or neutral without feeling, as long as both the company and customer recognize it as such and accept it on those terms.

> **Not all love relationships with customers must be passionate, love-at-first-sight conflagrations.**

Mismatch in love type. Consider, for example, companies such as banks, insurance firms, or newspapers, where most of the business comes from long-term subscriptions. Management at those kinds of companies tends to neglect their old and loyal customers. They may offer gifts to attract new customers, but they usually forget about those who provide the core of their business.

If an angry subscriber were to approach the company by calling his service center and threatening to leave because of neglect, he may receive a similar introductory gift. But it may already be too late. The company may have already lost his trust—and his business. What happened? The company showed only habitual love to this long-time subscriber, while he responded with passionate love, trying to get them to pay attention to him.

Common but neutral love type. What if a customer says that she doesn't expect any special treatment from her bank since all banks are really the same? That is a neutral love. It is a love relationship that will continue as long as both parties aren't investing any effort in the relationship. And it will continue until another "lover"—or bank—comes and woos the customer away.

Feigned love. Feigned love may be the most dangerous type. The company and its employees give the impression of courting and wooing the customer, but in reality, they could care less. At the same time, there are customers who may give the impression of loyalty just to get a special offer while looking elsewhere for other suggestions.

Private-label substitution love. When customers buy a private label item of a particular chain, whether it's a can of soup or a shirt, they want to convince themselves that the chain probably buys its private label products from major manufacturers. They don't want to believe that the product was actually made and purchased for very little in China. They are seeking substitution love.

Degrading fake love. Similarly, degrading love is when the consumer, knowingly and willfully, buys a product that is inferior, such as cheap hot dogs or a fake Rolex watch on the streets of New York, to impress his friends with his nouveau riche style.

Despite the many different types of love, real or fake, most serious manufacturers make honest efforts to achieve passionate love relationships with their clients. For this, they invest in research, advertising, promotion, and marketing, trying to reach consumer hearts and their utmost loyalty.

The Brand Love Ladder: Six Steps to Infatuation

When Selecting the Type of Love, Consider the Brand Love Ladder

The ancient *Kama Sutra* provides us with an elaborate description of the necessary steps for achieving passionate love: "Just as the sun's heat makes butter melt, so, when love melts reason, affection is formed. With increasing affection comes consideration. When consideration grows, confidence appears, and when confidence is full, passion develops. When passion reaches its highest level, it is known as infatuation" (121).

While many companies might only satisfy certain kinds of love, the real question is how can they achieve the one highest love, passionate or infatuated love? The answer lies in understanding the type of desire being sought.

A woman generally enters the wooing stage of a relationship looking for an ideal partner. She rationally and logically defines the character and traits of her ideal husband. However, the courting process is emotional and unplanned, full

> The courting proces is emotional and unplanned, full of unexpected surprises that catapult her into strong emotional and sensual experiences.

of unexpected surprises that catapult her into strong emotional and sensual experiences. She experiences the Love Ladder:

THE BRAND LOVE LADDER

| INFATUATION |
| PASSION |
| TRUST-CONFIDENCE |
| CONSIDERATION |
| AFFECTION |
| REASON |

Melting logical barriers. The Love Ladder happens to correspond to many modern marketing theories. The customer enters the shopping process with logical and cognitive definitions of her needs—with a reason. However, reason leads only to conclusions, whereas emotions lead to action. With the right wooing process, marketers try to melt her logical barriers, bringing her to develop affection for a brand or product that she may not have previously considered. This might happen because of a pleasant scent, attractive packaging, or a clever or affectionate sales clerk. If the attraction is strong, she will give the product serious consideration. The stronger the consideration she develops and emotional treatment she receives, the more confidence and trust she will develop for the brand. Only after

> The customer (woman) enters...with logical and cognitive definitions of her needs—with a reason. However, reason leads only to conclusions while emotions lead to action.

> With the right wooing process, marketers try to melt her logical barriers.

her confidence is maintained will she let herself develop a passion for the brand.

The more intense her passion, the more infatuation she develops for the brand. This is when she reaches the level of loyalty without barriers—having climbed the Love Ladder. It's a process that takes time, a series of purchases, and a period of using and appreciating the product.

Surprisingly enough, there are very few companies that measure passion or love in their customer satisfaction and loyalty models.

Anti-loyalty launches. In cosmetics, the opposite is true. Marketing managers complain about low customer loyalty due to customers' endless search for better and more advanced cosmetics. Yet to keep up with their competitors, cosmetic companies compound the problem by creating frequent product launchings and new, state-of-the-art chemical formulas.

One wonders whether these companies are too hasty in making their own products obsolete. The race to launch new products and brands, by definition, will never create customer loyalty. This race will always force prices higher in order to support research and development as well as pricey launches.

Perhaps management has been too busy launching new products instead of developing real emotional relationships with customers. Could they instead try to help their customers correctly use the most recent product, developing trust and, later, passion and loyalty for the product and the company?

> …Companies are so afraid of long-term commitments that they change frequently in order to avoid [them].

One has to wonder whether the companies are so afraid of long-term commitments that they change frequently in order to avoid it.

Affection, Passion, or Infatuation?

Marketers must decide which rung of the ladder they would like to focus on, which level of love are they striving for. Is it just affection, passion, or infatuation? If companies and marketers are going to show customers their love—whether passionate, infatuated, neutral, or any other kind of love—they must use the tools at hand to show that love. If they are going to help them climb the Love Ladder, they have to use the Sensory Star to draw customer to product or brand. They must classify and segment their customers, and then personalize the process; they have to show them the love.

No Skipping

*The order to be followed is determined by increasing confidence.
One thing must be done after the other: It is not possible to do
everything at once. (120)*

Marketers must remember that infatuated customers can't be created with just one trial use. There are no ways of skipping any of the rungs of the Love Ladder.

Recognize, compensate for, win. Going back to the concept of new segmentation criteria, we can now bring it all together. In our efforts to recognize, compensate for, and meet a woman's age, physical needs/traits, and temperament and desired type of love, we create winning marketing solutions and success.

For example, given women's physical and hormonal changes during different life stages, women seek products that can meet their current, specific needs. A woman of regular hip size and large chest wants accommodating bras and may require alterations when she buys clothing. A salesperson who recognizes those needs is able to reassure the customer with the appropriate solutions and win her loyalty.

Love for Love

But beyond the salespeople, marketers who address those needs will also win their customers' hearts, even if they only offer a sense and not actual proof that they're trying to solve those kinds of problems. And the women who feel they've been helped, or at least paid attention to, will offer their love in return.

> **Marketers who address those needs will win their customer's hearts, even if they only offer a sense and not actual proof that they're trying...**

This scenario brings about a new terminology in marketing: Love for love instead of merely value for one's money.

> **Women who feel they've been helped, or at least paid attention to, will offer their love in return.**

4. Four New Segmentation Specific Examples

Here are some examples of segmentation specialization in which marketers could win many Brownie Points:

1. Started in 2003, Not Your Daughter's Jeans (NYDJ) is a multimillion-dollar business that ships more than forty thousand pairs per week to two thousand stores in twenty countries. NYDJ has found an excellent adaptation to the following quote from the ancient *Kama Sutra*:

> *When their sexual drive is similar [regardless of size], a couple is well matched. (94)*

It is an excellent example of an effort to take the adult women's unattended physical features and convert those into a feminine advantage, giving the woman jeans that "flatten your tummy, lift your butt, and allow you to wear one size smaller." The secret to the tummy tucking is not only in the fabric content but also in the type of denim weaving, now patented, which constrains the stretch in the front and also gives the rear a lift. The fit stays comfortable but allows most women to buy a size or even two sizes smaller than normal. And a dream comes true!

2. Most food or cosmetic experts know that women of different age groups have different metabolisms, requiring different minerals, food supplements, and vitamins. Why not produce different food items that cater to each age group, labeling them by color, sign, or logo according to segmentation? Just as there are breakfast cereal selections for the mature woman—Special K's "pinch an inch" cereal, for example—manufacturers could put a special logo on all products produced for the mature woman.

Unilever in the United States, the Netherlands, and Belgium has recently launched the "My Choice" label. The label certifies that levels of sodium, sugar, and saturated and trans fats do not exceed standardized limits and claims that this "first-ever standard global front-of-pack stamp ... will help make it easy for consumers to make healthy choices."

3. The need or desire to lose weight is widespread among modern women. It's well-known that 95 percent of women who go on a diet end up returning to their original weight. Women realize more and more that lifestyle—including diet and exercise—is more important than sticking to a specific diet. A person looking to lose five pounds has different needs than someone who wants to lose twenty pounds. For example, she will not need new clothes, unlike a woman who loses twenty to thirty pounds. Further, those who wish to lose ten pounds live differently than those who wish to lose twenty pounds. They wear different clothing, have a different social life, may approach entertainment and shopping in entirely different moods, and look at themselves through a completely different lens.

Why not develop a new language, a genre with terminologies appropriate for different weight-reduction segments? Companies can create food products with different color labels for people aiming to lose different amounts of weight. This follows a new trend that Kraft Foods is currently embarking upon in its labeling system. Instead of merely listing calories, it's also using its labels to tell how the food was cooked, which gives more information to the buyer—whether they're interested for dietetic or health reasons.

4. Each year, the women's magazine *Marie Claire* announces the top ten cosmetic products according to their technical and marketing scale. The competition, Prix d'Excellence, is considered the Academy Awards of the cosmetics industry. The selection committee is composed of dermatologists, plastic surgeons, opinion leaders, journalists, and marketing experts. In 2006, one of the first nominated products was Platinum by Lancôme, a special cream for women over sixty. As one of the judges said, "Finally there is an end to the taboo. Beauty has no age; the skin has changing needs."

Chapter Three

Kama Festivals
Valentine's Day for Brands and Their
Customers

The amusements that take place at the festivals for the eighth day of the moon, at the spring festival.... The women who come to the city market are invited as a group to visit the apartments of the royal palace. (368)

Just as Valentine's Day, a day of love on February 14, was created to promote marriage between lovers, Kama Day (or Kama Festival) should mark the day when organizations and their lovers (their clients) reciprocate their love and commit to one another in marriage. This could be either a day selected by each organization or, perhaps somewhat megalomaniacally, by all organizations and the clients they love, creating a worldwide Kama Day. Organizations can invite the women in the marketplace—especially their loving wives—to visit their festival, harem, parties at the beach, park, or food fair.

Action—Part Two

In your marketing activities, remember that wooing never ends. It starts before the purchasing act (the Preludes) and it continues much after the act (the Conclusions). Once a marketer has selected the appropriate niche and the suitable type of love he wishes to activate in the consumer, the appropriate mix of sensory stimulation must be researched and created. By thinking differently, by thinking sense-ually, marketers can revolutionize how products are sold and who buys them.

1. Adopt the Love Mix Theory, which encompasses both preliminaries and conclusions. This means that your wooing should start at the store level and reach the customer at home while she is using the brand.

2. Exploit as many senses as possible throughout the entire brand experience. Decide what percentage of your customers make buying decisions inside the store, and accordingly activate your Love Mix on initial promotion, on point of purchase, and on actual use of the product. Consider using a Love Mix manager, preferably a woman, to work with your different brand managers (based on the probability that most will be men).

3. Plan an optimal sensory star:

- Select the appropriate senses to exploit.
- Decide on amount and relative strength of each sense.
- Plan a different sensory star for each contact point with the customer (in store, in use, etc.).

Force yourself to exploit at least one new sense. If you now utilize only touch (package design) or sight (labels, logo, or advertising), try adding smell or sound to your Sensory Mix. Organize internal contests and engage your employees in originating new ideas for your new sensory mixes.

4. Create, execute, and follow up on a Sensory Plan (the soul together with the mind).

5. Study—constantly and in-depth—your brand's BUYER pattern. Be a fly on the wall. Conduct an after-purchase research study to establish how the product is actually used by the household's different users. Does it satisfy their needs? Do they know how to enjoy its functional benefits? Use anthropological techniques to observe your clients where they use the brand. Try to reconstruct the emotional experience through conversation (see part 1) if you can't actually observe in-home use. Follow your customers' reinforcement process before and after using the product. One way is to open forums on the organization's Web site.

5. Create loyalty teasers. Along the different stations of the BUYER challenge, help the baffled client develop brand loyalty by capturing her in her house and encouraging her to use the brand when she really needs it. A good example of a loyalty teaser is advertising messages that remind users how thirsty they are and and that they should put Coca-Cola in the fridge. Loyalty teasers should also induce the dissatisfied client to complain and express her dissatisfaction rather than let it build up internally until she decides to quit the brand.

6. Create appropriate brand-extension policies. Let your loyal customers share your decision to come up with brand extensions. Do not rush to launch new products in a particular category before you make sure that most consumers feel they have finished using the previous brand and are ready for a new extension.

7. Establish where your clientele is positioned on the Brand and the Organization (Reciprocity) Love Ladders. Decide which rung of the ladder you wish to focus on—affection, consideration, or passion? Once you choose the type of love you wish to activate, declare it to your clients.

8. Adopt new emotional segmentation of your customers. The original *Kama Sutra* provides many interesting ways for new Kama Sense Marketing segmentation, including:

- age,
- clients' physical relevant features, and
- type of love that fits your brand's and your customer's expectations.

9. Study carefully those three spectrums and come up with new kinds of segmentation. When it comes to emotional segmentation, try to select segmentation factors that could be traceable and reachable rather than general and hard to reach. Traceable and reachable segmentation could be:

- Women who are overwhelmed with their efforts to lose ten to twenty pounds.
- Women over fifty who wish to change their lifestyle along with their hormones intake.
- Near-sighted customers who can't read your labels or instructions.
- Women who have trouble finding an appropriate match for a specific physical characteristic they have.

Once you decide on your emotional segments, it will be much easier to adopt the appropriate Sensory Mix.

10. Consider the possibility of assigning a special manager for different age groups; a manager for the 50+ women will be able to better understand their needs and devise better communications.

Part Three

The Marriage Vow in Marketing
Marrying the Customer

Chapter One

Why to Marry in Marketing

Once marketers adopt the philosophy of love, it is only natural that they will also accept the concept of marriage as the ideal frame for securing longevity of relationships with their clients.

Without love, marriage has no purpose.(270)

In Kama Sense Marketing, the marriage goal is to assure love between the brand and its clients for a long period. In romantic love, a man woos a few women but ends up marrying only one (or two). In Kama Sense Marketing, the marketer woos many, but ends up marrying only a few!

> **In Kama Sense Marketing, the marketer woos many, but ends up marrying only a few.**

Marriage in marketing should be the goal of all client-brand relationships. It's an ideal for both the client and the organization. In Kama Sense Marketing, the ultimate goal for every emotional brand is marriage to the loving customer.

> **The ultimate goal for every emotional brand is marriage to the loving customer.**

Aims of Marriage in Marketing

"Marriage can have three aims: pleasure, procreation, or virtue."
(224)

These three aims, slightly modified, can be easily applied to Kama Sense Marketing.:

Pleasure. The customer's pleasure from the buying transaction has two elements:

> 1. The sense of warmth and security she gains from fulfilling the never-ending consumer desire to make the right selection and from the confidence and trust she absorbs from the familiar brand or service, which makes her life more efficient and secure.

> 2. The emotional and functional benefits derived from the product itself.

A client recently described how she felt while reaching for her favorite brand of instant coffee on the supermarket's shelf and putting it into her shopping cart: "I reached for it instinctively, with very warm associations. It's similar to meeting an old friend. I was just thinking that I could hardly wait to get home and have a cup of Jacob's coffee."

A happy marriage could generate a lot of pleasure to the organization too. A loyal wife pumps up the organization with more volume for fewer costs, leading to better profits, stability, and consistency. This stability results in profits and stock-value increase, earning her the status of "Valued Customer."

Procreation. The second aim of organizational marriage, procreation, derives from the generation of new customers created by the buyer's commitment. The "spouse" promotes the organization and its brand through word-of-mouth networking and recommendations, while the loving client happily extends her experiences with the organization's new brands and products that help improve her standard of living by using the brand continuously.

Virtue. Finally, both organization and customer gain from the organization's genuine statements and promises to love its employees, the community, and its clients (see part 1). That promise and show of love and affection will provide immense gratification to both the marketer and his wife—the customer.

In Marketing Too, We Need a Marriage Act

In a traditional romantic relationship, the culmination of the wooing and love declaration is the moment when the couple officially, publicly, and cognitively decide to commit to one another and announce their marriage. They fix a date and a location and sign a "contract" between them. It is a formal act agreed to and pursued willingly by both parties: "I now pronounce you man and wife."

> Marriage is a cognitive and rational process in the midst of an emotional relationship (ecstasy).

Marriage is a cognitive and rational process in the midst of an emotional relationship (ecstasy). I have often wondered why the same process does not exist in marketing, as the official mutual declaration of a commitment and emotional bond between the husband and the wife. Just as a woman brought her dowry, together with her love, to marriage, the customer brings her financial endowment (purse, credit card,

> Just as a woman brought her dowry, together with her love, to marriage, the customer brings her financial endowment...in addition to her love and loyalty.

and checkbook) in addition to her love and loyalty, to the buying relationship.

But the pursuers of the reciprocity theory would rightfully ask, "What does the organization offer in return?"

Chasing the client. Marketers will need to recognize their customers as permanent lovers in their lives and announce their status on their own initiative and not necessarily as a result of an active request from the customer herself.

> Marketers will need to recognize their customers as permanent lovers in their lives and announce their status on their own initiative.

Unlike frequent-flyer clubs, credit card memberships, or department store membership clubs, where the customer makes the effort to register (and sometimes even pays a registration fee), the company or organization will be the one chasing the client. In existing membership clubs, one senses that the customer needs to constantly prove her worthiness, receiving gifts and gestures only when she deserves them because of the purchases she has made.

The time has come for a new type of personal relationship, as the following examples demonstrate.

Penthouse or platinum club? Mr. J. Bay, like many other affluent clients of XYZ Bank, had enough capital to be selected for the platinum club. The club catered to those who deposit a minimum of $500,000 or more, and platinum club members enjoy the benefits of being courted and wooed by the bank's personnel. One day Mr. Bay, on the spur of the moment, was offered the opportunity to buy a large penthouse near the waterfront that he had always dreamed of owning, necessitating his withdrawing a large amount of cash from his account. He planned, at the end of the few weeks it would take him to sell his current home, to replace the amount withdrawn. During this time, his bank balance dipped below the net deposit required to enjoy the benefits of platinum membership. The bank refused his explanation, and Mr. Bay was summarily removed from the platinum program without any consideration that his cash flow problem was only short-term.

Although the bank's behavior sounded logical, Mr. Bay found the incident insulting and degrading. Such behavior considers only a value-for-money relationship, not a value-for-value philosophy, and definitely not love for love.

The Oldest Client. At the end of 1992, I was granted a project by one of the largest Israeli banks to qualitatively analyze what constitutes a good branch manager. I went to interview a manager who was described by the bank CEO as one of their best. I began our conversation by asking him in what year his branch was established.

He looked at me curiously and answered, "Although I've worked here for only four years, I believe that the branch has been around for no longer than fifteen years."

"Please name three established business customers who have been with the bank since its inception," I said.

He gave three names without hesitating: Company AA, Company BB, and Company CC.

"And how long have each of the three been working with this branch?"

He looked at me with a smile, as if beginning to enjoy the game: "I believe that they have all been with us for around fifteen years, since the opening of the branch."

I then challenged him to check those numbers with his secretary. About ten minutes later, his secretary called back to say that AA has been with the bank for sixteen years, BB for fourteen years, and CC began working with the branch in 1962.

There was dead silence in his office. The branch manager hadn't even been aware that his branch had been in operation for thirty years. He didn't lose control but immediately picked the phone and called the manager of CC. After a short exchange, he told him to open his calendar because he would like to invite him for lunch at a fancy local restaurant. The CC manager thought that the bank manager had lost his mind. "What happened to you?" he asked.

"Mr. S., congratulations!" answered the bank manager. "We are celebrating your 30th anniversary with our bank and I would like to take you out to lunch."

The manager of CC, baffled, then told the bank manager that he was now going to invest $1.5 million in an employee pension fund through the bank. He had initially decided to invest the lesser amount, $500,000, after protracted negotiations with the bank, and had just told his secretary to call the bank with the news. But after the bank manager's phone call and recognition of the company's years as a customer, he was changing his mind.

It had taken only a few minutes of the secretary's time and one phone call from the branch manager to show the client how much the bank really loves and cares for him. The bank branch manager had announced to the loyal Company CC that he was "pronouncing them man and wife."

Building Databases

Database mining versus speed. As with the case of Company CC, organizations can easily mine their databases for loyal and heavyweight customers eligible for commitment and marriage. I recently asked a manager of a call center that sells books by telemarketing whether they can tell how many books a particular customer has purchased during the last twelve months just by glancing at the computer screen when the customer calls. The manager said yes, but when I asked her if their service personnel use this information when interacting with the customer, she said no, that it would impair their transaction speed and efficiency.

Attention, respect, trust, then love. What is missing in marketing is the public act of matrimony and its pronouncement that X customer and Y marketer are committed to one another. This act of recognition and commitment gives female customers a sense of attention and respect and promotes trust and eventually love.

> What is missing in marketing is the public pronouncement that X customer and Y marketer *are committed to one another.* This… gives female customers a sense of attention and repsect, and promotes trust and eventually love.

Organizations should build their databases with the intention of seizing every possible opportunity to indicate their valued buyers' candidacy for marriage by actively showing them how much they are loved and cared for.

London "On Us." Whenever I visited London, I used to ask my travel agent to book me at the Stratford Court Hotel, a few yards from Oxford Street. I'd always liked the hotel for its small size, convenient location, and personalized service. During one of my many visits, I returned to my room to find a fruit basket and a letter signed by the hotel manager. The letter read:

Dear Mr. Levy,
Our records indicate that you have visited our hotel 10 times in the past. I am happy to inform you that during this visit, your stay will be on us.

With this act, the hotel management had pronounced our marriage. I kept returning to this hotel and until, unfortunately, the hotel was purchased by another chain and changed its name and style.

New Year's Gift. But other examples exist. My assistant Adi spent a few years in Australia, where she subscribed to Vodafone cellular services. A heavy talker, she received a New Year's gift package from Vodafone. She opened the package to find one of Erickson's newest cellular phone handsets, free and unconditional on any future purchasing, as a sheer token of appreciation for her loyalty. This is definitely a marriage pronouncement!

The Reciprocity Love Ladder

Before going into the rational and tedious procedures of organizing the marriage ceremony, the organization needs to make sure that its client feels that the organization or its brand really loves her in return. After administering the Brand Love Ladder, which measures the extent to which the customer loves the brand, it is now appropriate to measure the Reciprocity Love Ladder, which measures the extent to which the client feels that the brand or the organization loves her in return. This could be surveyed by building an average weighted index based on the following six statements, each measured on a five-point verbal scale:

1. Their sales environment and their sales staff always make me feel good.
2. They offer gestures and gifts every time I buy or use their brand.
3. Whenever I approach them, they indicate that they really know me and my needs.
4. They really care how I use the brand after I buy it.
5. Whenever I call, they give me the feeling that they really love me as a client.
6. They surprise me with gifts and gestures even when I don't buy the brand.

THE RECIPROCITY LOVE LADDER

| SURPRISE WITH GESTURES |
| SERVICE WITH LOVE |
| CARE HOW I USE THEIR BRAND |
| WHEN I CALL THEY KNOW MY NEEDS |
| OFFERS GESTURES WITH PRURCHASE |
| FEEL GOOD IN THEIR SALES ENVIRONMENT |

It is the sixth scale of the Reciprocity Love Ladder that analogizes the marriage pronouncement and the act of marriage. On one hand, the organization has to single out the client who, through her behavior or attitudes, indicates her love for the brand, so that the organization can now reciprocate with love, unrelated to the purchase or use of that particular brand. This is what marriage in Kama Sense Marketing is all about.

> **With this ceremony, the organization can now reciprocate with love, unrelated to the purchase or use of the particular brand. This is what marriage in Kama Sense Marketing is all about.**

Since the need for these gestures is continued and repetitious, there is a need for a better term for importing the marriage act into the world of marketing. The ancient *Kama Sutra* came again for help with its creed for a marriage vow, or the Matrimonial Vow.

The Matrimonial Vow

> *When a marriage is celebrated … it includes a rite called Septapadi, in which a husband and wife make a reciprocal vow.*
> *(287)*

To clarify intricate and sensitive relationships without causing confusion to any side, Vatsyayana recommends a sort of an emotional vow, to be taken by the two sides.

Whether the wife is an only wife or one among others, marketers and clients need a vow to define their emotional relationship. Although some marketers will counter that for years they have been operating under a "service pact," the Kama Sense Marketing vow is more than a pact. A pact is more of a legal document agreed by the parties: You will buy my brand, and I will guarantee product functions and service. A vow, on the other hand, is a solemn pledge by each of the two parties to continue and contribute to the emotional relationship in a festive tone and with gala. This vow will dictate the basic duties of each of the two parties involved.

Kama Sense Marketing vow. Instead of detailing how many units the wife must buy for recognition as the "only wife" or as the "chief wife" (as most buying clubs do), the Kama Sense vow should state how this particular wife adds long-term profit to the organization. She does this by not inducing costs and by recommending the brands to others—both activities contributing to the benefit and welfare of the organization.

Getting in return. There is nothing wrong with a vow that includes such a statement: "We promise to do everything to convert your encounter with us into a long and a positive emotional experience, and we would definitely expect you to recommend our brand to your best friends. We will constantly prove to you how much we really care for you and for your needs."

Chapter Two

Whom to Marry?

A man cannot marry all the women he woos. During his bachelorhood, he may woo many but end up marrying only one (or several). The same applies to Kama Sense Marketing.

If we use the marriage analogy in marketing, then organizations will become polygamists. Most marketers would like to marry as many wives as possible—the more the merrier. And there is nothing wrong with that—as long as each wife receives proper attention.

Confronted with such new tasks and opportunities as befits men aiming to get married, marketers are going to need a better and more meaningful definition of who and what a customer is and which customers are eligible for becoming a wife.

Who and What Is a Customer?

Not all of your customers are worth marrying; not all clients are loyal customers, and not all loyal customers are lovers of the brand. Not all of your customers even want to marry your brands.

Jacob Levy

When a customer is asked in a conventional survey what soft drink she last bought and she answers Pepsi, does that mean that she is a Pepsi lover? Or just an occasional Pepsi buyer? Most books, articles, seminars, and professional discussions on marketing define those they wish to attract emotionally in a rather ambiguous way, as those who buy from the organization without any qualifying factors or value recognition. This is why the term *customer* always needs a qualifying adjective attached to it, such as a "loyal" or "steady" customer.

Five Customer Emotional Levels

We need better-defined terminology for customers and clients. Let's dismantle the term *customer* and divide it into five emotional levels: buyers, clients, loyalists, lovers, and wives.

Buyers buy the brand without any distinctly emotional attachment or repeat purchase. A buyer can be a woman who buys the brand for the first time or an occasional buyer without any particular attachment to the product.

Clients are more personalized. They buy the brand with some regularity as their main brand but may also buy other brands in the same product class. They begin to appear in the company databases as repeat customers.

Loyalists are clients who have already developed some emotional attachment to the brand. They buy the brand or the product because it makes them feel good and because they trust it more than any other brand on the market.

Lovers are those clients with loyalty beyond boundaries—what we have termed "the infatuated" in previous chapters. They love the brand or product so much that they are proud to use it. They may wear its name emblazoned on shirts or watches, tattoo it on their skin, and they certainly tell everyone that they should also buy this brand. They are keen advocates of the brand.

Yet these lovers can only become wives if and when the marketer initiates the marriage pronouncement actively. The lover customer has committed to the brand and its products; the organization now needs to do the same—to reciprocate.

One important way to discriminate between a loyal client and a potential wife is that wives are really looking for a stronger connection with the brand. I remember a case when a woman told me, in an in-depth qualitative interview: "I really love this brand, but I would like to be left alone. I don't want to be bothered." This definitely indicates a loyal customer that is not interested in marriage with the brand.

Who Is Worth Marrying?

Thanks to their investigations, one is able to know of any apparent defects that could mitigate against an alliance. (219)

The above customer categories define the different types of clientele in terms of their emotional engagement with a brand. But the categorization could go further. Smart organizations should augment this classification with some financial criteria. We need to always remember that love does not stand alone; and it also needs wealth and virtue to realize its full potential.

Emotional Categorization + Financial Criteria = Valued Customer

Who is a valued customer? An organization's marketing plans usually describe target customers in terms of who they are, what they think or feel about the brand, and where they can be found. But these target customers are not generally described in terms of whether they are worth marrying.

Who really contributes to wealth and welfare? They are not necessarily defined in terms of how much they really contribute to the organization's wealth or welfare. Kama Sense Marketing recommends considering marriage only to customers the organization wishes to attract and who would love to be wooed by the organization, creating a marriage that will yield prosperity and satisfaction for both sides.

Clients, Yes; Troublemakers, No

> *If she has a bad reputation, is secretive, breaks her word,...*
> *disobedient, immoral, is agitated ... she should be rejected.(221)*

Perfecting the selection process would enable organizations to detect and attract clients who bring more volume to the business and to shy away from troublemakers who may only increase costs. The organization should learn how to distinguish troublemakers from value makers.

Compulsive complainers. Many service centers can easily identify customers who are compulsive complainers, who crowd the service centers with nagging complaints but contribute little to organizational volume, adding losses to the organization. Efforts should be made to identify them and offer them other solutions. Maybe they shouldn't be chased away, but they should definitely not be considered eligible for marriage.

Currently heavy versus latent heavy buyers. Following the Pareto theory of 20 percent–80 percent, in which 20 percent of all customers contribute 80 percent of all volume sold, should we marry only our currently heavy buyers? Definitely not. Many in the market can be defined as "latent heavy," that is, able to increase their purchase of the same brand (or of other brands within the organization). Organizations should try to marry those who contribute to the enjoyment and the ultimate value (the wealth) of both parties—the consumer and the organization—and not merely to total volume.

How does the consumer contribute to her own enjoyment and wealth? Merely by buying or using brands that she enjoys, that give her emotional satisfaction, or that improve her standard of living.

Value for value, not value for money. This brings us back to the notion of "valued customer." The Kama Sense concept isn't just about volume but about value; that is, it's about valued customers who contribute to the organization's long-term profits as well as to its sales. How does the customer contribute to the long-term profits? By generating word-of-mouth advertising or simply by buying more of the same brand or of other brands of the same organization.

We're reinforcing the creed of "value for value" instead of the conventional "value for money." The process goes like this: At first, the client receives and contributes value to the organization or the brand. This means that both get from this experience something more than just the purchase itself. If this value is further magnified by emotional stimuli from the organization, the client receives emotional benefits as well. Finally, with Kama Sense Marketing, the arrangement becomes "love for love."

Chapter Three

Three Cs: Contact, Content, and Conversation

We will describe the preparations for organizing a meeting with a view to obtaining the girl.(217)

Full emotional confrontation. The marketing person must find the right occasion, location, and language for a full emotional confrontation with the client that will eventually lead to marriage. In practice, marketers are faced with three new paradigms in the matchmaking process, summed up as the three Cs: *contact*—where should the wooing take place, *content*—what to say, and *conversation*—how to say it.

Contact—A Personal and Direct Confrontation

Internal versus External Contact Opportunities

How can a man, without assistance, seduce a girl from a good family, in order to marry her by simple reciprocal commitment......, and how can a girl attract a boy of superior

status and of serious mind, in order to make him her husband?
(260)

Vatsyayana suggests various ways[to obtain the girl], which are of
two kinds, external and internal (260)

These two, the internal and external, are not merely physical criteria. They also have philosophical and psychological connotations requiring different approaches, signs, and techniques of wooing.

Internal meetings. In the internal wooing scenario, the suitor has the stage and the audience to which he can exercise all of his intimate performances. The girl can grant him her fullest attention, and vice versa.

In Kama Sense Marketing, this could take place when the client comes for a visit, at the company's store, at bank branches, or when a service man visits the client's home and can project in his behavior the organization's code of ethics. At these encounters, the clients are more attentive, interested, and open to information, persuasion, service, and flattery. Wooing for marriage from internal sources is more direct, concrete, to the point, and honest.

External meetings. In public, the wooing situation is altered because of the various audiences in the area. The lovers have to speak in cues and hidden signals in order to stand out from the crowd and to draw individual attention to one another.

In Kama Sense Marketing, when customers visit an exhibition or the cosmetics floor at an elegant department store, each brand fights for the consumer's attention. The organization might find a way to understand her gestures, direct her to the right shelf, suggest a brand trial, offer needed brand information, and so on, before beginning to discuss the actual purchase. An organization may seek customers through external sources, such as trying to make a personal contact with its occasional buyers or trying to attract nonbuyers through networking, advertising, or point of sale. To attract an occasional buyer to become a client eligible for potential marriage is to use an external source, since most likely, her record will not appear in the organization's databases. She will therefore not have been marked as a valued customer.

Occasions and Locations

Any suitor, once he has made up his mind about the woman he wishes to marry, needs to seize every opportunity to see and woo her. Some opportunities to meet will come his way naturally; other situations and contexts must be devised in order to move the courtship forward. The *Kama Sutra* describes the different locations where such meetings can take place as well as the activities and interactions that must happen at those locations.

The *Kama Sutra* recognizes three major locations, or matchmaking stations, at which the man and woman can first meet:

- the suitor's home,
- the girl's home, or
- public places (e.g., parties, ceremonies, or the Web).

Contacts in the Kama Sense Marketing

The ancient book recommends different techniques for meeting and matching depending on whether the date is intimate (internal) or public (external).

Active or Passive

The organization can be either active or passive in seeking customers from either internal or external sources, depending on the initiator. When the client approaches the organization, seeking service or repeat purchases, the organization is rather passive. But when the organization makes an effort to reach existing, service-silent customers, those who don't call the organization because either they are satisfied or they are fed up and on the verge of switching to the competition, it is active.

Passive contact opportunities. Most service organizations are mostly aware of and passively preoccupied with those clients who choose to actively contact the organization. Relying on this approach, they neglect the service-silent clients.

Active contact opportunities. Unfortunately, active internal occasions for interacting, although well defined, are not abundant. Most of the active internal occasions are initiated by the clients themselves. They tend to take place in situations in which the organizations are passive, merely reacting to clients' calls. It doesn't have to be that way. Business organizations have a wealth of unexploited opportunities for match making with new clients (and, later, for commitment pronouncements). Modern marketers know how to develop efficient customer relationship management (CRM) call centers and how to perfect their points of sale (POS) or point of purchase (POP). When developing more personal and emotional relationships, organizations need to exploit these many points of contacts.

Organizations' databases, if used correctly, could provide many opportunities for selecting potential marriage partners and for making marriage pronouncements. In Kama Sense Marketing, the internal sources exist in the form of databases that accumulate from frequent contacts with clients and loyalists.

The above conditions apply also in Kama Sense Marketing. After deciding to actively pursue a particular client, the marketer should not miss any opportunity to meet, in person, with his sweetheart in order to advance their relationship. Some of those opportunities will come his way naturally in the normal course of business (most of those initiated by the client who contacts the organization for service or a complaint), but some will have to be invented by the marketer to push the relationship into a successful marriage. A little brainstorming goes a long way in coming up with new ideas for finding time together.

Potential Emotional Meeting Points in Kama Sense Marketing

The concept of different places of contact, internal or external, indoors or outdoors, intimate or in public, is easily applied to Kama Sense Marketing. Kevin Roberts, in his new book, *The Lovemarks Effect,* claims that in Attraction Economy, two places matter most: on screen and in store. Using the insight provided by the *Kama Sutra,* we could easily accept that there are more than two.

The following list summarizes some basic contact points in most organizations that could easily be converted into emotional matchmaking locations. This list of contact opportunities is currently highly valued by data miners as information generators. Here the list appears solely as potential meeting points, at which organization personnel could depart from their daily routine to take a little extra time to express emotions and love. Here are the three basic potential meeting points for the marketers:

The Organization Environment

- Inside the company's store
- Call centers and customer service branches
- Letters to the complaints department
- Company's Web site

The Customer's Environment

- At home or place of use
- Technicians and service personnel visits
- Internet

Public Places

- Advertising (on and off screen)
- General chain's store
- Internet

The Organization Environment
Inside the Company Store

Glances and Hearts. Enough has been said about the importance of an appropriate sensory atmosphere at the point of sale and about how to treat female customers. Here we're dealing with more-intimate encounters with customers with whom the organization is seeking marriage. These are already clients, loyalists, or lovers of the brand. In these kinds of intimate, face-to-face encounters, we should follow the ancient text that recommends the encounter take place in the glances and hearts of the two parties.

> The true union will be when their glances—customer and marketer—will be satisfied along with their hearts. This is the essence...of emotional branding and the Sensory Star.

> The visual connection... is not enough for a long, healthy marriage. There is a need to engage the heart as well.

The true union will be when their glances—customer and marketer—will be satisfied along with their hearts. This is the essence behind the concept of emotional branding and the Sensory Star. The visual connection, either through advertising or product design, is not enough for a long, healthy marriage. There is a need to engage the heart as well.

Some opine that fortune comes when their hearts and glances are united. Otherwise it would be better to renounce the marriage.
(221)

Missed Loyal Clients. When loyal customers or even advocates browse through the aisles of one of the global fashion chain stores, the following events may take place:

- Nobody from the store personnel recognizes them despite their importance to the store management.
- They do not receive any special help during their visit to the store, although they may have needed it.
- While browsing, they do not know what special promotions the store is offering them on that particular day.
- If they are recognized at all, in most cases it is at the end of the visit, at the cash register.

In short, their loyalty to the chain doesn't receive any reinforcement, and the store may lose sales if these clients need explanation or help. If recognized at all as valuable customers, it is only at purchase time when they reach the cash register and present their club membership card. In a sense, the store doesn't show those valuable clients how much it loves them.

Internal tracking. For purposes of the marriage ritual, "lovers" should be recognized when they enter the store or the service area, and not only upon departure. This requires a sophisticated internal identification and tracking system.

Toyota test drive. I consider myself to be a loyal lover of Toyota cars. I'm currently driving my fifth Toyota in a row. For the last twelve years I have driven only Toyotas. Last year my wife was contemplating the purchase of Toyota's Rav 4. We approached the appropriate clerk to conduct a test drive and the clerk told us that there was a wait of three months. On the day of the test drive I asked the salesman whether, on his computer, he could detect my history and special standing with Toyota. Without even checking, he replied negatively, pointing out that his current software does not enable him to view a client's past record with the company. How many more sales could Toyota have made if its salespeople could recognize and welcome their loyal clients once they enter their store?

Client info for competitors. The situation is much worse in cases of FMCG, where the manufacturer has no contact with the client in the store and most of the client information goes to the food chain owners, who can utilize it for their own advantages (for example, to advance their own private labels). FMCG marketers need to find or create primarily external and active strategies for meeting their potential clients.

Call Centers and Service Departments

Call centers and service departments are love nests—potential places or opportunities for converting sheer service into love relationships. Organizations receive thousands of calls daily for information, inquiries about new purchases, service requirements, and complaints. Those are all opportunities for an emotional contact with the client. Service people, for example, could bring a flower or piece of chocolate for the customer.

Furthermore, the organization's software should be able to instantly track and identify the customer characteristics of each caller:

CRM (Customer Relationship Management): Ms. Buyer, congratulations! Our records show that you bought your first car with us exactly ten years ago. On behalf of our company, I want to send you ...

Experts in CRM know all the tricks and are already teaching service personnel how to transform an angry customer into a lover. However, we are mostly interested here in pronouncing marriage to those who have been defined as valued clients. For example: Ms. Buyer calls the service center to complain that her new washing machine is giving her trouble.

CRM: Yes, Ms. Buyer, we will gladly send you our technician. By the way, how is your dryer? I see that three weeks ago you filed a complaint about your dryer (provided that they indeed have such a tracking system). Is it working OK? If you don't mind, I'll ask our service man to also check your dryer this coming visit.

The organization has proven to the client that they track her needs and that they really care for her.

Buenos dias. In most cell phone service centers, clients are asked to take a number and wait their turn in line for the service personnel. What if, upon entering the store, the client could punch in his cell phone number so that the organization's database could identify him and assign him the appropriate service category and maybe even the appropriate clerk (for example, Spanish speaking, same gender, etc.)?

Letters to the Complaints Department

Sometimes they pretend to quarrel, seized by sudden anger, then changing their behavior, they become loving and affectionate again.
(201)

Lover's quarrel. Behind most letters received by the complaints departments are lovers—customers who care for the company and its brands. I would dare suggest that the head of the complaint department always assume that behind each letter of complaint is a hidden lover; otherwise, they wouldn't have taken the trouble to sit down and write a letter. Therefore, each complaint could also be considered an opportunity to deepen the relationship and push for marriage. Sophisticated customer-relations personnel know very well how to convert those complaints into a love-and-marriage relationship:

> *Dear Ms. Buyer,*
> *It has been brought to my attention that about two weeks ago*
> *you sent us a letter complaining about the way our service*
> *department had handled your call about problems with your*
> *washing machine. I am just calling to find out—has the problem*
> *been solved to your satisfaction?*

I would even suggest that, in some cases, marketers initiate the complaints—perhaps by openly asking clients about problems they have faced with the organization—and seize such opportunities for deepening emotional relationships.

> *During a game, the lover should start off some difference of opinion,*
> *giving right to a violent argument. In this case, the way he seizes*
> *the girl's hand is the same as when the betrothed takes his wife's*
> *hand during the marriage rite. When he takes her hand this way,*
> *the girl realizes that he wishes to marry her. (260)*

Honest complaints. One of my clients, a manufacturer of refrigerators, reorganized his service division to improve customer satisfaction. A few months later he came to me complaining that the number of complaints has almost doubled since his reorganization. It didn't take me much to convince him that this increase is a sign of trust and love because his clients now truly believe in the honesty of his service.

Company's Web Site

- Women use forums and bulletin boards relatively more frequently than do men, and their use of the Internet for creating communities through such media is rising rapidly.* (*Wikipedia "Gender Differences")

Feminine Web. If gender marketing is an accepted concept, then why not the feminine Web? The feminine or gender Web would be a worldwide community catering to women's needs, language, culture, and society. The Internet could then serve as the main location for satisfying the basic women's needs of conversing, consulting, sharing, talking, shopping, recommending, fantasizing, and whatever else—all in the convenience of their home or office and with minimal interference. When they are together, women find it generally easy to talk about anything and everything. Recent research suggests that, in a normal day, a woman uses an average of 20,000 words, while men use only 7,000 ("The Female Brain" - Louann Brizendine). Other research suggests that women's messages in Internet forums are longer than men's and that women use more emotional terminology; men use more rational and cognitive words, such as democracy, nations, software, Microsoft, gaming, programming, and economics (Neilsen-BuzzMetrics).

Company Web site. The organization's Web site is where the organization has some control over content. Marketers need to make sure their Web site is especially fitted and geared for women, reflects their special needs and moods, is free of all pop-up ads, is easy to manage and use, is written in warm fonts, and has appropriate music and sometime in the future, the right scent.

Buying through the Internet

Just as buyers in the bazaars will not purchase an object without seeing it, a marriage can only be accomplished if she has been seen and appreciated.(266)

Buying through the Web alone isn't sufficient. Some retail chains enable their customers to select their products—whether clothing, shoes, jewelry, electrical appliances, linens, cosmetics, or anything else—online, and the vendor offers to send the items to one of the stores closest to her. This lets her see her selection in person before she decides to buy. The retailer acknowledges that meeting the woman only online is not sufficient; this contact needs to be supplemented with a more personal contact.

How about developing a chain of small fitting rooms, scattered geographically, where customers who buy through the Web could visit and see, try out, or try on items they had bought through the Internet from different suppliers before actual delivery?

For a successful Web-based organization, I recommend that marketers meet their customers not only through the one-way focus-group mirror, but also in one-on-many sessions in which top marketers meet and talk with their customers, guided by a professional, targeted, and experienced moderator-coach. This setup will require female mentors developed inside the organization, with dedicated lines of communication to female clients. These dedicated lines will allow the female mentors to speak in their own, personal, female language, catering to their customers' moods and needs.

The Customer's Environment
At Home or Place of Use

Marketers tend to forget that products are purchased mainly for use outside the store environment, according to the product function and the client's lifestyle (the kitchen, the toilet, the car, or social gatherings, etc.). In most cases, the client is left alone at these important moments, when the product is supposed to justify its purchase and live up to its functional and emotional expectations (or to the BUYER challenge discussed in part 2). And indeed, when the customer is left alone with the brand, in the daily intimacy of life, brands do talk! Perhaps the customer curses while taking a shower when the heavy liquid-soap container slips from her hand to the floor.

Library-shelf cereal. Breakfast cereal manufacturers are very well-known for their marketing and research sophistication. They are experts in brand and package labeling and product promotion. On the supermarket shelf, their brands' facings (the front two-dimensional package graphics) activate the appetite of children and adults alike. And yet, in a recent anthropological survey conducted for a global cereal manufacturer, we noticed that in one home visited, all cereal boxes were stacked on the pantry shelf on their sides, making it impossible to read the front labels that usually appear on the store shelf.

One of the family members, a twelve-year-old boy, felt like preparing his favorite cereal. He opened the pantry door to find six boxes of cereal stacked on their sides. All he saw was the list of minerals and vitamins, which he did not understand or care about. He couldn't select his favorite brand since they all looked alike and the name of the brand didn't appear at all on the side of the package. Somewhat angry and hungry, he started pulling down each box, one at the time, like selecting books on the library shelf, trying to find the front label of his favorite brand.

The most interesting part was that by doing this he ended up selecting a different brand than the one he was looking for. His favorite brand had not completed the marketing assignment and found a way to label the side of the package attractively. Although marketers may do much to help the client select the brand on the shelf, they may do little to help the client use their brand at home, incurring the risk of losing "stomach share."

Technicians and Service Personnel Visits

In most organizations, the service department is completely unconnected to other divisions and especially to sales and customer care. Moreover, most service or repair people get paid for completing their client calls—whether in repairs, installment, training, or other areas—as quickly as possible. In the Kama Sutra Marketing era, the separation between service and other organization departments will change. Every employee or even subcontractor of the organization will be obliged to see the emotional side of every customer call.

Bezeq and bonuses. Some years ago, I did qualitative research for Bezeq, which at that time was Israel's only landline telephone service. Bezeq had a rule that installing new telephone sets in new customers' homes should take no more than twenty-five minutes. Technicians who adhered to this rule received a bonus, and those who didn't were penalized. At the end of the week, a supervisor noticed that one of his technicians had spent forty-five minutes on a simple installation. Angry, he demanded an explanation.

The technician explained that the customer was an elderly woman who lived alone and had asked him very nicely to explain the different functions of the new set and how she could use it in her daily activities. The service technician told his supervisor, "Maybe I lost a bonus but Bezeq won a happy customer." When I interviewed the technician, he told me he didn't think that his supervisor understood.

Mr. Clean syndrome. Since Procter & Gamble introduced the masculine symbol of Mr. Clean in the late 1960s, I sense that technicians who visit customers at home at least subconsciously see themselves as the image builders of their organization's desire to pamper its female clientele and as solicitors for the next purchase. This is especially true in the Internet era, in which many customers meet only the technical staff of the virtual organization from which they buy products and services. I call this the "Mr. Clean Syndrome." Wikipedia describes Mr. Clean as: "a muscular, bald man who cleans things very well. According to the company, his image is supposed to be that of a sailor, although most people think he is a genie based on his earring, folded arms, and tendency to magically appear at the appropriate time."

Although technicians and service people may be the only people from the organization in personal contact with the client, some don't really make an effort to project anything other than the reason for which they were called. Others try to sell some other related brands, but very few really try to create a new experience to glorify the brand.

Hollandia plants. At home we sleep on one of the Hollandia International electric beds with an engine that lifts up each part of the bed on demand. Whenever we call the service people, the technician arrives with a small plant and with a large smile on his face, which gives us the assurance that everything is going to be okay.

Internet

Women's natural game. In addition to the organization's Web site, the World Wide Web provides excellent matching places for the brand to meet potential lovers eligible for marriage, such as forums, blogs, Facebook, Twitter, MySpace, and Youtube. The most probable would be an active blog of another woman with similar needs or with similar brand experiences.

Public Places

Marketers should constantly look for new opportunities for emotional matchmaking. Until now, I have mainly described customer-initiated contacts, whether through a service call, a letter of complaint, or the company Web site. Now it's time to discuss organization-initiated contacts. Here again we distinguish between pursuing the masses for general marketing and wooing only a few choice customers. Those particular clients who are singled out will love it when the organization, out of the blue, surprises them with some justified and relevant gesture. And the creative mind is limitless.

FMCG loyalists. A producer of FMCG (fast moving consumer goods) sends a special supervisor to visit the homes of heavy users or loyalists to discuss usage problems and future opportunities in the different categories, not only for learning about their products but also to declare loudly to their loyal customers, "We care about you and would like to learn from you."

Lunch with advocate. Repeat buyers or heavy users (depending on the category) can be invited to lunch in a luxury hotel in order to treat them, but with minimal sales talk. At the same time, each table should have at least one advocate or lover of your brand in order to engender a positive feeling for both new customers and loyalists.

Networking instead of advertising

In order to form an opinion about her, people must be found who are connected with her father and mother and, for the purpose of this inquiry, the views of friends and persons who frequent the house should also be taken into account. (218)

Still the most important tool for reaching other customers in this day and age is, of course, networking! One should use networking either to learn about the potential prospects or to arrange the first meeting and eventually the wedding ceremony itself. "Friends may also be used if they have some relationship with the two parties" (219), and even "the servants views should not be overlooked" (218). The matchmaking process purposefully avoids the discussion of advertising as a point of contact. As emphasized earlier, mass advertising is primarily one-sided, with a passive customer—not allowing for any real intimate or interactive relations to take place. For more intimate contacts, networking is recommended, particularly because it was used very effectively during the times of the *Kama Sutra*.

Physical signs of intentions

When the boy and the girl find themselves side by side in some place he must give her physical signs of his intentions. Words serve no purpose. (260)

Physical signs? Yes, a familiar concept to us in the marketing world. In Kama Sutra Marketing terms, the package, advertising, gifts, samples, and any other physical symbols of the brand or product are definitely part of the *Kama Sutra*'s "physical signs of his intentions." It is always a challenge for marketers to conceive of new and different physical symbols to attract the attention of the target clients. The original *Kama Sutra*, with its list of 64 arts of love, could spark many such new ideas for the curious and creative reader: flower bouquets, jewelry, head ornaments, lace making, and so on.

Content—What to Say to The Client

We have the contact locations; now we need the content. It is not enough to create contact opportunities. Each opportunity must be filled with the appropriate emotional content.

It is a challenge for marketers to learn how to decode the buyers' signals when they are given and to know what to say during those intimate meetings. Do they know what language to use? What should we talk about in order to induce the girl into matrimony? Remember, we would like to create events that will show our valued and loving client how much we love her in return and that we would like to declare our relationship "man and wife."

Brandiversary

Some may suggest giving our valued client gifts—that this should do the marriage trick. Well, it will not! Gifts without reason or connection to an emotional event will be looked upon as a giveaway by an organization that apparently makes a lot of money. The solution is the Brandiversary concept.

Brandiversary is software that flashes information onto the computer screen regarding meeting places between the client's history and lifestyle and the brand's or organization's anniversaries and story. It is where the histories of both parties meet in a meaningful and positive way:

"Ms. Buyer, are you aware that our brand X was launched on your birthday exactly ten years ago?"

"Ms. Buyer, are you aware that, during the last twelve months, you have contacted our Web site more than any other client, and for this and for your good suggestions, we are sending you ..."

"Ms. Buyer, I have looked through your file and found that you have upgraded your cellular phone handset with us five times in the past. This time we would like to grant you a free upgrade of your choice."

Here are some examples of what the Brandiversary software can flash up:

- Birthdates of all of the client's family members.
- Other personal or family anniversaries of all kinds.
- Contact history with the brand or the organization (the number of years and exact date since Ms. Buyer started buying the product or started having contact with the organization).
- Corporate anniversaries. Do they match any of the client's dates?
- Important events or milestones in Ms. Buyer's relationship to the organization. She was the first to try a product innovation, and she usually buys the largest variety of the organization's brands.

The organization can also track important contacts or complaints concerning the product. The organization databases could be supplemented by adding questions that measure emotional needs of the customers from the interaction with the organization and its brands. Then by the process of fusion, it could help the organization segment its clients according to emotiongraphics.

The Future: A Heavier Personification and Characterization of the Brand

We should consider the possibility that women customers, the wooed, would demand to know more about the character of the wooing brand. Exemplifying its liberalism, the ancient book is eager to remind us that in marriage, a female has the same rights as a male: "A girl should find a husband whose character matches her own" (262).

Bearing this in mind, I envision a time when women customers will not be satisfied just by the act of wooing and will be interested in knowing the character of the wooing brand. Thus, this renders the brand personification as a genuine request and a precondition, as indeed the case with the recent campaigns of Pepsi "Max It" or with Axe/Lynx deodorants.

Some Words on Astrology and Her Mood as Content Potential

Astrology is underused and overlooked by marketers as both an external and internal means of attracting lovers and loyalists. Thanks to technology, we can supplement the Brandiversary with additional elements such as "Astrology and Her Mood."

Marketing classification tool for matching. The *Kama Sutra* refers to astrology, but mostly as a means for a better match: "It is only after having established the concordance of the signs of destiny, the moment's omens, and the position of the stars that the girl may be given in marriage" (220). In marketing, we can still adopt the softer role of astrology: "The grounds for choosing are of two kinds: from the human point of view and from an astrological point of view" (218). This suggests that astrology should come only after all other relevant options have been considered.

Classification, attention getting. Astrology should be explored as a marketing classification tool in the matching process as well as for attention-getting advertising or loyalty teasers, whether during selling or reinforcement. For example, the buying-mood concept (see part 2) is an excellent opportunity to use astrology. A woman's mood has a great influence on her purchasing decisions. This mood may be influenced by events that affected her that day, the time of day, or the season of the year, as experts in gender medicine suggest (Their claim is that most modern medicine was created by men mostly for male patients without taking into account the feminine hormonal structure, and it is about time that female patients should be approached differently). If women are willing to believe in astrology, why can't a specific brand manager direct his particular marketing messages to Virgos or Libras on a particular day of the week or month? I take this opportunity to call for straightforward research to discover if there is any relationship between astrology and the customer's shopping mood.

A recent poll I conducted indicated that 60 percent of women read their horoscopes regularly, and yet I can't remember even one case in the last forty years in which a client asked me to cross-reference the results of his research with the horoscopes of his respondents. Even if a marketer doesn't believe in astrology, isn't it enough that his customers may be curious about it? Again, specialized software will be needed to implement horoscope-slanted marketing, showing the customer's astrological sign while on the phone with the marketing professional. However, the ancient text had a warning on this issue: "Their [the signs of the zodiac, etc.] importance must not be exaggerated, nor should it be thought that every action in this world depends on them" (39).

There are various ways for utilizing astrology in marketing:

1. Add an astrology section to the organization bulletin, newspapers, or Web site, keeping it somewhat light but interesting to most women.

2. Ask women customers if they would like to know how different products apply differently according to the zodiac or astrology sign.

3. Keep astrology as another classification variable without any commitments. For example, "Our research indicates that Leos drink a lot of Pepsi during the summer."

Conversation—The Emotional Dialogue

Conver-sale: No More Sales Pitch

The most suitable contact opportunity using the best software will still not provide the desired results without resorting, ultimately, to conversation—the emotional dialogue that can help create sales (conver-sale), provide service (conver-serve), and acquire knowledge (conver-search).

We have all learned the importance of the sales pitch. The concept derives from baseball, where the pitcher and the batter are opponents in a war of deception and curveballs. In Kama Sense Marketing, there is no room for sales pitches. We need a new positive language, in which the goals of the sellers and the buyers are to meet and not to oppose, in which the two talk and listen to each other, look at each other, and are sensitive to one another's signals—in which there is *conver-sale*.

Conver-serve: Passive to Active/Positive/Emotional

Imagine that, when some client calls, the clerk could immediately see on his screen the client's relevant history and use those events to create an emotional experience with her. Creative and well-trained staff could easily convert each customer's call from a passive to an active and positive emotional encounter and eventually into a successful marriage.

None of these ideas alone can make a successful match and love-based marriage. This is why organizations must bring love into their strategy and mission statements. To this end, organizations need to acquire the appropriate language and tone for inducing the customer into the appropriate matching mood. (Louann Brizendine, MD, in her book, *The Female Brain*, emphasizes the importance of tone and language to women and explains the difficulties in measuring it.) Which again brings us back to research and acquisition of emotional knowledge, of Observe and Converse.

Conver-search – A new kind of research

A man who is trying to conquer a girl expert in the sixty-four arts does not arrange a meeting without first getting information.(217)

If he were living today, Vatsyayana would most likely be a researcher and consultant of love. Throughout the book, he repeats the importance of acquiring knowledge in order to improve relationships and immediately follows with the practicalities that evolve from research: "Having interpreted the state of her feelings from spontaneous signs, he must contemplate the ways of marrying the girl" (248).

In Kama Sense Marketing, the possibility of developing love relationships and successful marriages with the right clients depends upon correct information. Acquiring emotional knowledge begins with keen and attentive observations, such as learning her body language and interpreting the slightest signal she might offer.

Chapter Four

Matchmaking in *Kama Sense Marketing*

An intimate selection process. In most ancient societies, selecting a wife was rather simple. A wife was chosen through a matchmaker or through an agreement between the two families to make a match of their children. In contrast, the ancient *Kama Sutra* describes at length how a suitor should seek the bride of his choice.

Matching Must Be Done on a Personalized Path

Mass matching: one-sided. Marketers today, accustomed to mass marketing, will naturally look for mass-matching tools. However, mass marketing and mass advertising are one-sided and consider only the organization's needs—a situation in which the client can't fully reciprocate. Let's not forget: marriage is a two-way street.

Individual, intimate matchmaking. Many marketers will argue that the combination of their advertising campaign (offline or online) and their brand's functional performance create a relationship language with emotional messages that tell the client just how they really feel about her. But Kama Sense Marketing's matchmaking doesn't work that way. The marriage and the matching processes are both individual and intimate, dictating that the marketer choose an eligible individual customer from the crowd and approach her by her name or with some common interest in mind.

Direct-contact marketing. Reciprocating emotionally requires an interactive, interpersonal relationship. To ensure a successful match or commitment ceremony, Kama Sense Marketing proposes direct and interactive communication between organization and client. Imagine direct contact through interactive mobile cell phones, Internet blogs and forums, and even personal meetings with selected valued customers! With Kama Sense Marketing, the wooer can look into the eyes of his fiancée and hear her voice; then she can see, hear, and feel the brand and the organization behind it. And for this, we need the three Cs described above.

It's not an easy task. Finding the right customers and constructing the most appropriate three-Cs strategy is not an easy task. The ancient book recognizes this difficulty: "It is evident ... that, in order to relax the girl, the boy should know female psychology" (238).

Success comes not from sporadic incidents but from tedious and repetitive efforts of the marketing team. Matchmaking activities should be planned and integrated into the organization's general strategy. The marriage act and procedures should be incorporated into annual marketing plans open to accountability with alternative tactical plans for achieving targets.

A loving and caring man may want to learn how to truly relax his woman. Yet men, even the most sensitive, will not have the same capabilities of reading women's minds, stress, and feelings as women would. Kama Sense male marketers can use professional women mentors to help them in approaching female customers for the matching process or in helping men conduct appropriate conver-sales with their female customers. This will be discussed in part 6 of this book.

But here I would like to cover the use of natural, free-of-charge matchmakers or opinion leaders for bringing together as many women customers as they can to try the brand they love so much. Either on their own initiative or after they were induced by the marketer, through the Internet, or through personal introduction, those matchmakers can be extremely effective in bringing new wives to the particular brand. I prefer calling those go-betweens or messengers, but not matchmakers because most matchmakers are paid for their services. In Kama Sense Marketing, opinion leaders do it for fun—not because they are trying to sell anything but because they love and are loyal to the brand. Their role is to glorify the brand and organization and to show the other brand's wives how using this specific brand will yield them a better life.

From the Go-Between to the Knitworkers

According to Vatsyayana, if one can, it is better to do things by one's own means. However, if there are difficulties, a go-between should be used. (327)

The ancient *Kama Sutra* identifies them as the go-between or the messenger. Those go-between women can come from variety of sources, but always from among the loyal customers, the advocates of the brand.

A woman whose attitudes and favorable behavior have been observed, but whom one cannot meet alone, can only be approached through the mediation of a messenger.

Accordingly, Vatsyayana allocates a special section ("Task of the Go-between") to the role of those important mediators: Intermediaries, messengers, go-betweens, and others. In marketing, too, we use a variety of mediators, from opinion leaders among women to paid coaches for male marketers. In Kama Sense Marketing, both opinion leaders and coaches usually favor only one of the two partners, and mostly the man (the marketer). They differ from matchmakers, who represent both parties, deal mostly in arranging first marriages, and do not facilitate adulteries.

Creating the Bond

> *Having established this bond between them, the go-between accomplishes her role. (354)*

The closest terminology that comes to mind is modern networking, where some gifted women use their connections and conversation skills to introduce the man (in marketing the brand) to as many girls as possible without getting compensated for their work. But even here, we have some basic differences. In romantic networking, the messenger's role ends when the introduction is made. In Kama Sense Marketing, the go-between role ends only when the introduction ends in a positive match, that is, in actual use of the new brand.

> *"Because the young girl lives isolated from the world and sees no one, her nurse undertakes to assist her out of affection" (263).*

> *"She will show the boy's qualities to his best advantage and try to make her fall in love with him ... She strives to put the girl into a favorable frame of mind, so that the boy's initiative will find her with no fears" (243).*

Marketers need to be extremely creative and innovative if they want to do it on their own, and if they encounter difficulties, this is where knitworking can be used efficiently.

Knitworking. The word-of-mouth concept is generally a passive one, generated by its own internal dynamics. In word of mouth, an opinion leader—most likely a loyal client who loves the product—decides on her own when, where, and how to advocate the product to others. Networking, on the other hand, is an active process, planned by an interested party—usually the marketer—for delivering to others the love message in real time. I have decided that the best name for this unique task is *knitworking*. Knitworkers are women who, through feminine qualities and attributes and through back-and-forth techniques, approach other women to knit a wide network of heavy users or lovers of the brand—the desired brand harem.

Knitworking is especially suited for the Internet era. Knitworking on the Internet, enhanced by womanly instincts and conversation skills, could be a very powerful marketing tool. A group of loving and involved women can mobilize the dynamics and energy of the group to the organization's benefits. This is compatible with the new trend called *New Media Marketing* (Wikipedia, July 2008):

> With the development of Web 2, new marketing tools are open for the business community. One of those ... is ... New Media Marketing.

> A relatively new concept utilized by businesses in developing an online community, which allows customer evangelists to congregate and extol the virtues of a particular brand. In most cases, the online community includes mechanisms such as blogs, pod casts, message boards, and product reviews, all of which contribute to a transparent forum to post praises, criticisms, questions, and suggestions.

> One of the primary arguments to promote New Media Marketing is the premise that traditional advertising is losing its influence on consumers. Backed by statistical evidence demonstrating a growing trend of consumers making purchasing decisions off Internet research and referral, these advocates strongly adhere to the notion that consumers are more inclined to believe feedback from like-minded peers than

corporate marketing verbiage dispersed through traditional television, radio, direct mail, or newspaper advertising.

In my opinion, the Kama Sense Marketing's "knitters" are uniquely different from the mediators discussed above, by being brand users pronounced by the organization as wives, recognized as part of the organization's harem, and charged with the task of convincing "other" wives to switch brands. Their goal is to increase the organization's harem by as many wives as possible, either offline or online. In this philosophy, organizations should have a special manager responsible for activating this very important harem.

Offline

Dinner with other wives. I recall one service provider who invited heavy users of competitive brands to dinner. For this purpose, he arranged round tables with ten seats each and made sure each table had a keen client, an advocate of his own brands. Those advocates were never briefed what to say. The organizer was sure that around each table, those wives would tell the other brands' wives, in a natural way, how much they love their inviting organization and its brands. And indeed the dinner was an unprecedented success for the organizers. About 40 percent of the guests expressed interest in pursuing a relationship with the host organization.

Unequipped naturally with those sensitive conversation skills, men have to be coached and mentored for this task—preferably by women.

The Ideal Messenger

"Messengers, by exchanging letters, messages of love, and mutual expressions of feeling, are one of the main instruments in the reciprocal experience and knowledge" (362).

The organization reciprocity love ladder's sixth stage (part 3-chapter one) requires that the organization should surprise his loyal customer with gifts and gestures even when she doesn't buy the brand. The messengers and knitworkers have an important role in this endeavor, either in planning those gestures, or in locating those customers and in delivering those gestures.

Adroit, Moderate, and Enterprising

In another place, the author of the ancient text describes his virtues: "The three main virtues of the messenger are to be adroit, moderate, and enterprising" (345).

Praises and secrets. The required traits of an ideal messenger almost dictate that the knitworker be a woman: "She must present herself as a virtuous person and please the girl [the wooed] with astute chatter, telling her tales taken from literature concerning the amorous relations of famous women and men's adventures with other men's wives. Furthermore, she flatters the girl, praising her beauty, knowledge, her generosity and virtues" (346).

Friendly first. When approaching another organization's wife, the knitworker should approach the girl wisely and first try to establish confidence and friendly relations with her.

Only after they have established a friendly conversation on almost any subject (both knowing what is behind their meeting but not discussing it openly) and only when the time comes, does the messenger unfold her purpose.

Having formed truly intimate relations with the girl, she supplies her with highly advanced information. She explains to her the secrets of magic words and medicinal plants that procure knowledge, beauty, and fertility. When her words have produced an effect, a trust is born. (361)

Positive Qualities of New Brand

Describing the boy's character in a complimentary manner, she mentions his prowess in love. She mentions how he behaves at the beginning of the act, during the act, and at the end. (347-8)

Only then, after convincing her of the disadvantages of her current engagement, can the messenger go ahead and talk about the positive qualities of the new wooer.

She describes in exaggerated terms the boy's ability in the 64 arts and his success with women.(349)

Never Met

Not knowing the other's appearance, without having ever met, one can still manage to imagine the other's aspect. This is why it is spoken of as "picturing at a distance." (352)

Apparently virtual and imaginary visual messages were in use some fifteen hundred years ago, however, in most case the personal touch of the knitworker is essential.

Indeed, can the knitworker succeed if the other organization's wife has never seen or used its brand? The *Kama Sutra* presents arguments among experts on this issue (pp 352–3). Those in favor opine that a networking messenger can succeed in attracting her even if she has never met the brand or tried it.

For Vatsyayana, the go-between's business may be carried out without their knowing each other and without having seen what they look like.(353)

Negative Information

Noting which faults upset her, she insists particularly on those very ones. (347)

When trying to attract other brand's wife, a successful knitworker tells negative stories as evidence of objectivity and as examples of what not to do. Of course, this is only after marketers have a chance to research and reveal areas where those wives are most susceptible to negative information.

Blemishing the husband. In trying to attract other brand's wife, a good knitworker can, with her feminine tact, at some point even blemish the wife's husband (346): "'With so many qualities, how did you manage to fall for such a husband?' In such a manner she inspires regret." Or, "Given your qualities, how did you get such an ugly husband?" and "You wonderful woman! Your husband doesn't even deserve to be your slave." (344)

Brand X versus slander. Before the '70s, TV advertisers showed how their brand performed better (smelled better, tasted better) than "Brand X." They avoided calling the competitive brand by its real name so as to avoid a lawsuit. Only in the '80s did TV advertisers begin to show commercials in which both brands—the advertised and its inferior competitor—were identified by their names (of course running the risk of a liability suit by the competitor).

In the *Kama Sutra*, this aggressive approach was used even some fifteen hundred years ago. The go-between wouldn't hesitate to attack the woman's husband by his real name. The trick was to find the right timing and dosage: She should praise the woman more than denouncing the husband. Only a woman messenger who knows how to approach another woman can say such negative things about the husband while praising the girl and the other man. The same applies to Kama Sense Marketing. Confronting the difficulty of convincing a wife of the negatives of the brand she loves and is loyal to, the knitworker should use skill and deep understanding of gender culture and anthropology.

Gift-Giving

Wrapping of messages

Various feelings such as desire, sadness, anger, astonishment, mixed with compliments, are written in the form of riddles on these leaves with which, without damaging them, he wraps his gifts. (353)

The ancient text suggests that the intermediary could bring the courted wife gifts wrapped by the suitor, indicating his feelings by the type of wrap used. Why can't the organization find the most appropriate wrap, which may even be more impressive than the gift itself? For example, a gift wrapped in one kind of paper would convey to the recipient hints of readiness for seduction or love, while the same gift wrapped in another paper would convey friendly care.

When she receives his gifts, she thus knows the boy's feelings.(353)

Messenger Replacement

When, through her mistakes, the desired result is not reached, the messenger lacking skill with words must be sent away.(361)

Mediators should be relieved of their duties upon completing their tasks or if unsatisfactory to the marketer.

Role of CEOs

Kings and ministers cannot enter other's people houses, since the manner of the powerful is observed and imitated. (365)

The people highest up, such as the organization CEO, would not necessarily participate in the wooing. Marketers must understand that not all women are ready to be wooed at all times, and they're not always interested in remaining loyal to one brand in a particular category. A woman may be buying on and off from a particular marketer without feeling committed to his brand. And then all of sudden, when her mood and the situation are right, she becomes willing to be recognized and titled as a client or even as a wife. Marketers will have difficulties tracking such women, but knitworkers can easily do it.

Maximum Care with the Willingness to Recommend

In our efforts to utilize ardent loyal customers recommending our brand to their peer group, we should be aware of a recent finding from a series of qualitative conver-search sessions on facial creams. It should be reminded that most brand equity and brand loyalty research models include a question on a customer's willingness to recommend the brand or product.

Same-Day Dara. In the midst of a heated conversation, one participant was asked whether she would recommend her current brand of facial cream to a friend or group of friends. This question stirred immediate and enthusiastic reactions from several women in the room.

"Are you kidding?" she responded. "When I like a product, I never wait for my friend to ask me for a recommendation. If I don't call her and tell her about my reaction to the brand immediately after the experience, then she isn't really my friend."

Her friend continued, "If Dara doesn't tell me about it the same very day, it means she really didn't like the product so much."

At that moment I realized that the question "Would you recommend ..." is passé and should be replaced by questions such as "Have you recently recommended Brand A to any of your friends?"

Introverted versus extroverted brands. Delving deeper into the different brand psychographics patterns in this particular group made me realize something else: There are some brand categories that women will not converse about with their friends. I call those "introverted brands": chocolate bars, fast-food chains, or any other product category that women are quite indifferent to using. On the other hand, there are categories that women feel obliged to converse about, such as facial creams, laundry detergents, coffee, and so on. Those I call "extroverted brands." Within each extroverted brand, women could have different discussion groups, "the Brand Sociogram." With one group, they may discuss what movies to see, and with another, what diapers to buy.

Action—Part Three

The marriage ritual is for those who have already been wooed and have made the first purchase. Now we need to sell our loyal customers the concept of lifelong marriage.

1. Be wholehearted and serious. Developing a marriage strategy for personal/emotional marketing is a major commitment. Don't get involved if you just want a customers' club or one-time promotion gimmick. You are entering a long-term, one-on-one marriage with reciprocal commitments.

2. Use the personal matching process to select an appropriate mate, a match that meets both emotional categorization and financial criteria.

3. First, you must accept that a potential marriage is an emotional event as well as functional and monetary. Accordingly, try to develop an emotional matching index. That, for example, can explain (through multivariate analysis) why people might say, "This is a product for people like me."

4. Develop the financial criteria for defining "valued customers," those who really contribute constantly to your organization's long-range welfare. Use your improved database to select your wives and get rid of troublemakers.

5. Manipulate the three Cs for a successful marriage (contact, content, and conversation). Assuming that in the previous part you have already decided on your target audience and your Love Mix strategy, now you have to bring it into a successful marriage. Now, you should use the matching process to bring you together for the marriage ceremony (ritual). It is time to be personal. No matter who from your organization approaches the bride, whether

---

in a conversation or in writing, the approach should be based on events that actually took place—proving that the organization really loves and follows the customer's experiences with it.

Contact: Decide on the main points of contact (POC) for encountering your potential marriage prospects. Naturally, those POCs will be internal, that is under your control, such as service points, sales point, and—why not?—accounting. Determine the type of personnel who will be interacting with customers at each POC and train them to conduct emotional encounters.

Content: Here you'll have to decide on the content of the gestures you wish to use as a marriage pronouncement. Decide how to glean this content from your databases. Find events and experiences in the client's life that could integrate with the history of the brand and the organization. The following examples may trigger your imagination:

> *Dear Ms. Buyer, our record indicates that you began using our services exactly ten years ago. We are very proud of that length of service. In honor of our ten-year commitment to one another, we are sending you and your spouse for a free weekend at an exclusive spa.*

> *Dear Mr. Retailer, I just discovered that last year you purchased the largest selection of items from our yearly catalogue. By this, you have proven your loyalty to our family of products. Accordingly, we are sending you a voucher for your entire family to a one-week stay in the heavenly resort of . . .*

Prepare a list of active initiatives regarding your client's emotional history based on your existing databases (remember that little things mean a lot). Do not relate those pronouncements to any specific purchase; otherwise, they will be considered a promotional gimmick. The marriage prospect needs to know that you care for her regardless of her last purchase. When feasible, provide your clients with questionnaires that augment your databases with emotional points—such as date of first purchase from the organization, personal hobbies (if existing database doesn't have it), and personal events in the client's history that may relate to the organization's history, brands, and more.

Conversation: **In the wooing process, conversations are strongly recommended. Only in conversation will we be able to learn about the customer's emotional status and needs. For this we will have to train our staff with conversation tools and techniques.** Whenever you can, conduct one-on-one in-depth conversations with some advocates of your brand, for the purpose of learning how to induce conversations in the particular category.

Try to establish the flow, experiences, language, and the sociometrics of the specific category under investigation in the course of conversation. One way of modern conversation is to develop and run a special Web site or blog that will speak to women in their language and according to their culture.

6. Do not underestimate the power of astrology. In deciding on your content or conversation strategies, the question arises: why not astrology? Include astrology questions in one of your general surveys to learn to what degree your customers would react positively to astrology-based marketing. There are many ways to use astrology in marketing:

Add an astrology section to the organization's bulletin, newspapers, or Web site, keeping it somewhat superficial, but interesting to most women.

Ask women if they would like to get deeper into astrology; for example, getting some monthly suggestions on what brands should be used by the different astrology signs each month or in general. This works better in some product categories than in others.

Keep astrology as another classification variable without any commitments. If your research indicates such, for example, you could say, "Our research indicates that Leos drink a lot of Pepsi during the summer."

Incorporate astrology maps with your different products, such as different bed linen (drinks, fashion) for different zodiac signs—either as an indication of her mood or as a trigger for opening a conversation.

7. Try to establish if yours is an extroverted or introverted brand. While conversing with your women clients, try to learn whether they like to converse with their friends about your brand (an extroverted brand) or whether they will use it without needing to share it with their friends (an introverted brand). Here are some possible questions:

- Have you discussed the category or the brand with friends during the past thirty days?
- To what extent are you interested in hearing or reading what other women have to say about this category or brand?
- Have you participated in any Web site, forum, or blog on this category?
- Do you remember recommending the brand to a friend during the last twelve months?

8. In today's marketing atmosphere, marketers' thinking must go through five stages:

- Accept that, in most categories, women clients are relatively more important and therefore should be approached separately in your strategy.

- Accept that not all of your customers are worth marrying and/or ready to marry you in return.
- Accept that women's moods, their decision-making processes, and their emotional world are still a mystery to researchers.
- Openly accept that women mentors (mentoresses) can do a better job of understanding women clients than do most men.
- Allow talented women to actively participate in your marketing strategy.

Part Four

On Maintaining Customers' Loyalty

The Brand Sisterhood

Once married to the man, how should the wife behave toward him?
This is known as the 'Duties and Privileges of the Wife.'(277)

"Duties and Privileges of the Wife," part 4 of the original *Kama Sutra*, is the shortest of all parts. To Vatsyayana it was all very simple: In family and in love life, women have many duties but only a few privileges. To him it was more important to list the wife's duties than her privileges, an attitude that unfortunately has not changed much during the last two thousand years. Even today, in many societies, modern women are still fighting for more privileges while struggling with their heavy duties: having a career, raising children, taking care of the house and kitchen, hosting guests, and pampering their husbands.

Time to change. In the new Kama Sense Marketing, the situation will hopefully change. In their relationships with marketers, wives will have many privileges but very few, although essential, duties. All they must do is remain loyal, more frequently use the organization's brands, and recommend those brands to others. In short, they must be brand advocates. Meanwhile, their privileges are as many as marketers can create and invent. In Kama Sense Marketing, the burden rests

> He (the marketer) has to invent new privileges…, detaching himself from the notion that clients deserve attention only when the actual purchase takes place.

on the marketer's shoulders. He has to invent new privileges that will take him out of the box, detaching himself from the notion that clients deserve attention only when the actual purchase takes place. He must show that relationships with the loyal customer continue long after the purchase. Thus, it will be up to marketers to make this part of the book thicker and fuller.

Jacob Levy

Harem, No; Consumer Club, No; Brand Sisterhood—Yes!

In order to ensure the fulfillment of their pleasure, procreation, and virtue, the three aims of marriage, customers need a fermenting community, where they can exchange experiences, express emotions, and obtain new information.

The *Kama Sutra* suggests the harem concept as the place where all wives enjoys their privileges and perform their duties. Modern marketers most likely will recommend the customer club membership. In my opinion, neither of the two fits the Kama Sense Marketing philosophy; in the consumer club, the wives do not receive a personal treatment, while in the harem, she does not get the appropriate freedom and independence. The Brand Sisterhood, in my opinion, is the best solution for bringing together a group of women who are somewhat similar in their marketing needs and behavior. It is where a woman has the right to require her privileges and can leave at will whenever she wishes. Nobody understands women better than women themselves, and women with much experience and wisdom can create the right atmosphere for a better match. This is mingling and networking at its purest.

Status of Wives

The man who possesses the girl either has no other wives, or else has a certain number of other wives dependent on him. A wife may therefore be of two kinds: the only wife or wife among others.(277)

In ancient times, the man had to decide whether his newlywed wife was going to be his only wife, a senior among many others, a junior, or one among equals.

In modern Kama Sense Marketing, too, a marketer's first decision is whether to give his individual client the feeling that she is his only wife, a senior among many others, or one of equals, all receiving the same privileges.

Only Wife. The "only wife" approach is unique in marketing and belongs to a few high-class services. The "only wife" strategy is already in place in private banking, where each platinum client receives individual, personal treatment across the board as if he were the only bank customer. When such a client is invited to meet her consultants, they all convene in a small conference room, giving this selected client the feeling that she is the bank's only client and hoping to win a lot of positive emotional mileage from such a client. In a focus group conducted for a private bank in Israel, one participant described her emotional experience:

> Whenever I visit my private bankers, I am invited to an empty floor with two nice-looking secretaries who approach me by name and invite me into a small conference room with two pots brewing for coffee or tea. There is no other person on the floor. I always ask myself, "Am I their only client?"

Gold to Black. When the credit card era first began, the gold card was aimed only at the better customers. However, bank managers were forced to be liberal in their selections and gave it to almost everyone. Then came the platinum card, and once again it was distributed lavishly to every client willing to pay the yearly registration fees. Then, once again, Amex had to invent the Black Card, the Centurion (with a $2,500 annual fee), given to only limited clientele. Amex Black Card holders boast that their card will provide almost anything they yearn for. While Amex Black Card is probably one of the most sophisticated and luxurious clubs in the world, it is not a harem. It is a very functional card that will bring you anything you want to buy; the harem will also bring you love and surprise you with little things that emotionally mean more.

Chief or Senior Wife

In marketing, the more typical case is "many wives." Here the marketer has two options: All wives are treated equally, or there is a "chief wife and the other wives."

Selecting the Senior Wife. The concept of the senior wife will apply in many selling categories, such as airline frequent-flyer programs. Airlines have regular fliers; then on top of those, some kind of frequent-flyer program, corresponding to junior wives; and finally, on top of all, some kind of platinum club. In a product based on new innovations, it may be wise to develop the concept of senior wife, assuming that this supports the organization's strategy. In some categories, such as basic cosmetics or over-the-counter (OTC) drugs, marketers may want to start first with small groups of advocates and opinion leaders, senior wives, who will help them carry the brand messages to the other wives. Or in the case of private banking, the marketer may want to give each valuable client the feeling that she is his only client.

Potentiating senior wives. The senior wife decision seems easier to understand and adopt and yet it is not fully exploited. The success of senior wife depends on (1) marketing category and (2) management philosophy. Most important is that those senior wives, either in their behavior or in their conversations, become enthusiastic advocates of the brand and spread its merits through positive word of mouth. For achieving this, marketers need to activate more positive emotional incidents in their personal interaction and encounters with their senior clients.

King David Club. I myself am a longtime and loyal King David Club member of El Al Airlines. Whenever I fly, I always fly El Al. Despite my 100-percent loyalty, I have never been personally approached by anybody to explain to me all of my privileges in this membership and how could they improve my life. Nor have I been shown that my loyalty is appreciated. I sometimes wonder if the airline puts me at a lower level on the Organizational Love Ladder by rewarding actual sales (a frequent flyer who travels many more miles than I do but who gives only 50 percent of his business to El Al) over emotional commitment.

From Senior Wife to Ardent Advocate

A devoted wife puts all of her trust in her husband, considering him in her heart as a god. She conforms at all points to his wishes. (277)

The strategy of senior wife among many seems relevant to most marketing campaigns, provided that emotional relationships are reciprocal and mutual. With careful and creative plans, marketers can reap from their senior wives a lot of word-of-mouth mileage; as the ancient text says: "She does as he does in order to demonstrate her devotion" (281).

> Her first duty is to inspire total trust in her husband. She must adjust her conduct and ways of behaving to her husband's ideas and, as far as possible, make it so that their two bodies have a single soul. To attain such a goal, their attitudes must be disinterested and identical. This is why the text suggests that the woman should consider her husband a god and worship him (285–6).

Those "valued clients" pronounced by the marketers as senior wives will have some additional duties, which—with a little inducement from the marketers—could yield additional customers through an active word-of-mouth campaign. But marketers should never forget that we are talking about a reciprocal vow in which women clients have duties and many privileges—a vow that is always key to the success of such a unique and selective campaign: "The husband, too, should consider his wife as the goddess of fortune in his house and respect her" (286).

The codes of ethics, the Dharma Shastra, tell us that prosperity and bliss dwell in the house where the wife is respected. (286)

Reinforcing Personal Marketing

Personal marketing is useful whether we are dealing with "only wife" or "senior wife among many." Marketers may be reluctant to adopt a personal approach in large markets because of its expense and therefore end up creating some kind of mass-advertising program.

Assessing practicality of the senior wife approach. For example, a leader in a particular category in a large country such as England may hold 50 percent of the market. If he wishes to increase his share by 10 share points to 60 percent market share, he would consider it only natural to embark on a national mass-media campaign. To such a marketer, the senior wife approach may be impractical and expensive. But if we try to translate the marketer's target into actual numbers rather than only in market share goals, the picture may look quite different.

The UK has about 52 million inhabitants and about 20 million households. Assume the product category is used by 25 percent, or about 5 million households. With the conventional Pareto law of 20 percent–80 percent, in which heavy users (20 percent of all users) contribute 80 percent of all volume, we have a target of about 1 million households. This means that an increase of 10 share points needs only 100,000 more heavy users. However, a late study conducted by Catalina Marketing Pointer Media Network among 54 million Americans on 1,364 brands discovered that on the average brand it is 2.5 percent of all customers that contribute to 80 percent of all sells, making the conventional 20–80 law passé.[*] At any rate, both targets can easily be achieved with modern personal marketing, data-mining programs, and the Internet. There are many product categories in which such an approach can be even easier and more practical, such as when

---

[*]   Neale-Mae, Donovan. "Engaging The Right Customers." Esomar's Research World, June 2009.

selling a specific car aimed at selected populations or a platinum credit card.

Equality among wives

A man who has several wives must treat them equally. He may not neglect some and put up with the shortcomings of others.(301)

Whatever the strategy, it should be publicly known to all clients, without any secrets or prejudices. To this end, many marketers need to change their thinking and behavior to avoid neglecting clients. For example, organizations such as magazines, cable TV, banks, and insurance institutions grant new subscribers worthy gifts—forgetting and neglecting old subscribers who

> **"Wives" should get always the best and worthiest gifts as well as the man's wooing.**

contribute most of the organization's profits. Just as in romantic life, wives should get always the best and worthiest gifts as well as the man's wooing.

Wifely Rivalry

If the husband shows greater affection towards one of his wives, it causes fights with the others. (291)

But marketers should beware of treating clients differently; nothing is more frustrating than when another client receives more favorable treatment:

Too old to count. Some years ago I conducted a yearly tracking survey for one of the largest global drink manufacturers. For many years, the client would repeatedly define the target audience as the sixteen- to forty-five-year-old age category. In one of those briefings, my colleague, a senior research analyst of fifty-five years of age, insulted for being excluded from the target population, raised the following argument:

It is true that two of my kids are users of your brand, but I am always the one who does the buying. I am the one serving it to my guests, who are all above fifty-five. My husband is a very heavy user of one of your brands, and he is over sixty. I simply buy them in boxes of 1.5 liters, and I am fifty years old, so why don't I count in your company targets?

The research director looked at her, smilingly. "Please don't be insulted; those are headquarters' instructions!"

A few months ago, I was gratified to learn that the same global organization had decided to include "above forty-five" in their target market, which concurs with the current philosophy of many advertisers, who believe in "the more, the merrier" strategy, which tries to increase sales from any possible source at whatever cost.

Marriage Fatigue

The more numerous the wives, the more the hero considers them
as a weekly fatigue. Often, he refuses to couple with the one whose
turn it is, and sends her away. (299)

Crisis management. Creating a category of chief wives could serve the organization not only in advocating the brand and its line extensions but in dealing with crises. This helps the marketers handle many customers at once.

If the husband decides that he wants peace immediately, he himself
must organize the reconciliation. (292)

When a crisis appears, the marketer himself must immediately attend to the situation: "Taking the chief wife aside and speaking to her without the others, he flatters her by assuring her that he appreciates no one as much as her" (292). The marketer assumes that the chief wife, in turn, will address the other wives. This procedure is particularly important and practical in the Internet era, inducing chief wives to enter actively into the organization's sponsored sites (forums and blogs) as advocates and conciliators.

Whatever he does, the marketer should always remember that tricks or deception on either side would simply never work.

A Personal Note

A humble word of advice for the ancient author of the *Kama Sutra*: Had Vatsyayana spent a little more of his writings on the privileges of the wives instead of just on their duties, he wouldn't have needed to write such a long chapter on how to seduce other men's wives. With more privileges bestowed upon them, those wives wouldn't leave their husbands for other men so easily.

Action—Part Four

This part refers only to the wives of the organization—those whom the organization has decided to engage on a personal level. The concept of the marriage pronouncement forces marketers to think about clients in personal terms. The wife should be ready for a long relationship, with few duties but many privileges.

1. When it comes to pampering your customers, think personal. Do not be complacent knowing that your wives get a lot of satisfaction just from using your brand. Committed wives expect to get much more from your brand—something more personal. It could be a nice letter, a telephone call, a personal gift on a specific personal occasion, and so on, depending on the creativity of each marketer.

2. Create a structural framework—the sisterhood—for making many wives happy simultaneously. **For this you may need modern technologies that would enable you to do so. This is where emotional marketing could be at its best.** First, decide on your sisterhood's size and type of treatment.

    A. Sisterhood size criteria

        1. Contribution to sales—how do you define your wives? Heavy users only? Top 10 percent of contributing clients? Those who buy the widest variety of your brands, regardless of quantity?

        2. Emotional segmentation—use the niche approach if you want to marry those who are emotionally engaged with the brand regardless of their purchase volume (see part 2). Make sure your segmentation

criteria are known to all and transparent, without any prejudices.

B. Sisterhood treatment

1. Make sure you satisfy all of your wives equally. Be transparent and equal in treating both senior wives and your many wives. The worse that could happen to you is that your wives find out that you discriminate between them—giving some more than others. Similarly, be careful of the "Weekend Fatigue" insinuated by the ancient text, which can force you to be dishonest and to use gimmicks.

2. Choose the chief wife approach in categories in which you own and control your customer list. Chief wives could be the best advocates of your brand and an easy way to spread positive messages to the sisterhood community in situations of crisis management or new-product launching.

3. Try to establish the senior wife approach through the Web structure in FMCG, where you don't have access to your mass audience. In blogs or in forums, you are better off utilizing the Internet in a creative fashion.

4. Write a marriage vow that expresses the emotional commitments of both sides. This will facilitate your relationships with many wives. There is nothing wrong if you add a paragraph suggesting that senior wives should take upon themselves, whenever they can, to recommend the brand to their friends.

5. Conduct regular, periodical satisfaction surveys among your sisterhood members.

6. Twice yearly, conduct a short emotional-satisfaction tracking survey among a representative sample of your sisterhood or general clientele, depending on your category and the type of relationship you wish to develop with your clients. Also, maintain a blog or company Web site in which you invite customers to openly discuss their emotional experiences with the organization and its brands.

7. Employ a new kind of group dynamics: sorority dynamics. Ask one of your brand advocates to invite a group of female friends to her house to converse on the subject under investigation, to induce loyal customers to spread their positive experiences with the brand. In the course of the conversation, try to establish the flow, experiences, language, and the sociometrics of the specific category under investigation. Induce those friends to converse as openly as possible, and introduce your questions into the course of conversation.

Part Five

On Seducing your Competitors' Wives

Chapter One

Preventing Your Wives from Being Seduced

The main aim of this work is to assure that women are protected.
(387)

Happily married men will prefer to skip this part of the original *Kama Sutra*. Most likely, they will not be interested in learning how to seduce other men's wives. However, in the *Kama Sutra*, "Other Men's Wives" is about three times longer than "Duties and Privileges of the Wife." Does this mean that Vatsyayana, the monk, prefers adultery over a sound and happy marriage? Not at all! Although he recognizes adultery as a natural part of life, he openly condemns all kinds of adultery. But Vatsyayana gives a convincing reason for reading part 5: "Being well informed by this book of the ways of having intercourse with other men's wives, a man who has understood the text properly cannot be deceived by his own wives" (386).

Marketers are interested in (1) how to protect their own wives and keep them from being seduced by others and (2) how to attract other brand's wives. The first is the easier task, provided that the marketer keeps constant contact with his wives. The second task, reaching other organizations' wives, is much harder. The ancient analogy suggests that when marketers treat their loving wives nicely and correctly, word could easily reach and affect other brands' wives.

Chapter Two

Whom to Seduce

Didn't marry—unlikely to seduce other wives. If marketers lack a solid strategy or programs for marrying their own selected loving and valued clients—that is, they do not commit internally with the matrimony vow—I doubt they will readily invest great effort to locate, approach, and marry those few but extremely valuable wives of their competitors.

In my experience, marketers are rarely willing to spend money on individual names or lists of other organizations' wives (loyalists). Competitors' wives are loyal lovers and heavy users who contribute most to the other organization's sales (assuming the Pareto Law of the 20–80). And they are hard to get. Under the influence of their advertising people, they would rather launch general, "one size fits all" campaigns to attract all sorts of customers, as long as they are category users.

You should always expect rejection when attempting to attract others' wives. Women may reject such efforts depending on their mood or their current situation. Married women can have many reasons for rejecting other men's advances. In most cases, such reasons are insurmountable and indicate the health of our society (spasmodic switching between women and adultery could be symptoms of decadence). Most of those reasons for rejection listed in the *Kama Sutra,* on page 314, could easily apply to marketing situations. To some organizations this gives optimism and, to others, pessimism. Here are the original quotes with their relevancy to Kama Sense Marketing:

- "She loves her husband." She is in love with the competitive brand and likely will not even notice other brands. This is when the organization calls its customers "committed."
- "She is mature." She cannot be easily swayed by other brands' cheap claims; she has passed this stage.
- "She has some current troubles." She is currently preoccupied; she is not in the mood.
- "She cannot manage to free herself." For example, in the cellular category, she might have a long-term contract with her current brand.
- "She is not approached properly." The new brand did not show her respect.
- "He lacks discretion in his wooing." This is a common error made by many overeager salespeople.
- "She suspects that he is without financial means." Clients prefer to do business with financially sound organizations.
- "He is not informed about local habits." This happens when global organizations think global and act global instead of thinking global and acting local (or even thinking local and acting local). There are many examples of cultural mistakes marketers make when penetrating a new country.
- "She despises him because he is of low extraction." This definitely applies to the nouveau riche customers.
- "He is stupid because he does not understand a sign and does not seize an opportunity." An overeager salesman does not know how and when to end his sales pitch and

start closing the sale.

- "Because he is old, she has no consideration for him." When and how to rejuvenate the brand is always a dilemma for an old and established brand.
- "Because of ethical reasons." She is under a verbal oath to use her current brand.

To expand on this theme from my own experience: In the databases of my current cell phone provider, I can be easily defined as a heavy user and one of their first clients, since I joined during their first week of operation. I consider myself a proud loyalist and have never considered switching providers. And although during almost ten years of this relationship, I was never approached by this provider with any sign of recognition of my loyalty nor with any sign of love, I don't consider switching to another provider.

If we remember that heavy users, the most important contributors to the category volume, are only 20 percent of all users in the particular category and that those are divided between a few competitors, then we will better understand why marketers prefer not to bother at all.

Wooing single versus married women. Wooing an unattached woman is completely different from seducing a married woman. It requires different techniques and approaches. I suspect that most marketers do not distinguish between first-time buyers and wives, either their own or those of their competitors, in their tactics or in their strategies.

Why woo competitors' wives? Banks as well as cell phone operators have a churn rate of no more than 10 percent who at any point in time consider switching to another service provider. Those 10 percent will be divided almost randomly among many competitors, and still all banks and cell operators spend bundles on advertising and promotion to attract all sorts of new customers. They could be much more effective if they would court and attract other brands' heavy clients.

Hard to Get

He does not esteem a woman who is easy to have, but interested in one who is difficult to obtain. This is a general rule.(313)

In romantic life, men by nature appreciate women who are hard to get. Most advertising campaigns are aimed at those who are relatively easier to get (that is, they are already users of the category). In marketing, as in romantic love, we need to also woo those who are difficult to get. Thus, in reality, if we want to attract heavy, loyal customers of our competitors, we must find them and understand their needs so we can give them a specific message.

The tobacco industry reached this conclusion the hard way. Because of regulations and strong legal limitations, they were forced to move to one-on-one, or direct, marketing. They accumulated huge databases of smokers of different competitive brands, which presented the organization with a wonderful opportunity to actively detect emotionally engaged and loving clients, get to know their lifestyles and needs, and accordingly offer them marriage.

Mass versus personal marketing. Trying to target small, select groups of other brand's wives who just happen to be ready for a switch is very difficult with current above-the-line (ATL), or mass-media, advertising and requires below-the-line (BTL), or direct/personal, campaigns. But marketers may shy away from the personal involvement of BTL marketing because of stricter accountability and less glamour. That is, in direct marketing and personal marketing, marketers can be held more accountable for successful results, which are much more apparent and immediate. Personal campaigns are also more difficult and less fun because they don't draw the large budgets that broadcast channels do.

By contrast, in mass marketing, marketers are less accountable for successful results. They can just show a beautiful woman driving a beautiful car for a broadcast campaign and offer endless excuses for why the commercial didn't work—other than the campaign lacked relevancy and inspiration.

> **Mass...marketers are less accountable for successful results: they can just show a beautiful woman driving a beautiful car...and offer endless excuses why the commercial didn't work**

Now with the help of the Internet and mobile phones, we may be able to market to individuals more easily. But first we will need careful research and planning.

Chapter Three

Need for Careful Research and Planning

An astute man manages to get his hands on another man's wife after developing mutual acquaintance, attaining a certain familiarity, and studying her mentality. (344)

If a loyal client is worth seven frequent buyers, then attracting another organization's wife is worth many more, but she is still almost impossible to get without special effort.

Understanding the Other Wife's Mentality

> If a loyal client is worth seven frequent buyers, then attracting another organization's wife is worth many more, but she is still almost impossible to get without special effort.

Not all women, or even most women, but only some women desire to attach themselves to other men, or are even capable of being aroused by this desire. For this reason, an understanding of a woman's state of mind is of the utmost importance. (344)

"To understand a woman's mentality, her behavior must be studied constantly" (329). The courting and seduction of other organizations' wives requires careful planning based on extensive and unique research. This research should differ from research on unattached single girls. Yet in my forty years of marketing research I have encountered few cases in which advertisers sought to explore the needs or habits of wives of competitors' brands.

Assessing Risk

In this connection, the possibilities of success must first be examined.
What risks are involved? Does she want to make love? And so
on.(309)

Although ad agencies may convince marketers to create new campaigns to bring in new customers, they neglect to warn that getting customers to switch brands is a mammoth job. We are talking about other men's wives. A customer entering a store is faced with thousands of choices, and she feels satisfied that she can purchase the brand she loves and does not have to go through the pain of making a selection. In trying to get the wife to switch brands, the advertiser may have a risky task and may get nothing for the trouble.

To minimize risk, research and plan carefully. Although research is constantly necessary throughout the marketing process, I must emphasize that it is most important to do research now. Wooing organizations might need to develop special task forces for locating, attracting, wooing, and converting those competitors' clients. As those activities require considerable investment of money and effort, marketers should constantly ask themselves:

> Although research is constantly necessary throughout the marketing process,…it is most important to do research now.

- Is it worthwhile?
- How long would our relationship last?
- What would I gain thereby?

- Would my new customers leave again for someone else? (Did they come because of my promotions, discount, or coupons? For pleasure or because of true love?)

Bear in mind that the emotional needs of the customer may vary from one competitive brand to another. For example, attracting wives of a large bank may require a different approach than attracting wives of a small bank: "One's behavior to her must be based on nature, through her appearance, expressions, glances … etc." (329).

Assessing Her Mood and Feelings

"Once contact has been made, the woman's state of mind must be studied, her feelings examined, ascertaining whether she is sure of herself and her resolution is firm" (337). Good research can also help discover the wife's state of mind, her mood, and her feelings.

Assessing Her Worthiness

"Before letting amorous desire take hold, he must first examine the woman's character, her physical aspect, the signs of love games on her body, which are indicative of her behavior, her faithfulness, purity, life, her blameless conduct, so as to decide whether the enterprise is worth the while" (311). Only with an efficient database and creative use of primary research can marketers weed out bad customers from valued, loving ones.

Assessing Her Appreciation of Emotional Strategy

"Some women are very enterprising, but lack temperament. For the boy, it is useless to amuse himself with such women: a woman who lacks sensuality is of no interest" (344). Because emotions and love will be at the base of your strategy, do not approach those who do not appreciate emotional relationships. As information technology (IT) becomes perfected and marketers become much more informed and efficient, I can foresee an era in which customers who do not show signs of appreciating their organization's emotional strategy will be rejected by the organization, as was recommended fifteen hundred years ago.

IT: Screen and Locate

The need for creative and innovative research is immense. Finding wives of other organizations is particularly difficult in fast-moving consumer goods (FMCG), as purchase data are controlled by the food chains, and manufacturers and advertisers cannot acquire names of either their competitors' wives or of their own lovers and heavy users. With IT advances, marketers should devise new technologies to screen and locate those important wives and develop special wooing plans for them. Seeking a small group in most categories, sophisticated direct-marketing campaigns should not be ignored. For example: A producer of a certain FMCG brand could call for all customers of competitive brands to send in ten empty containers of the competitor's brand in order to get five or ten new ones of the producer's brand for free during a period of one month (to ensure heavy usage of the brand). Such a campaign, along with creative use of the Internet, can help identify the competitor's loyalists or heavy users for further wooing.

Chapter Four

Wooing for Adultery

By means of repeated encounters, an indestructible relationship is created.(333)

According to Vatsyayana, to successfully seduce the loving wife of another man, three conditions should be met:

1. **Physical Meeting.** The woman should have a chance to see and physically encounter the man.

2. **Stronger Desire.** The woman's desire for a union with him should be even stronger than the man's.

3. **Patience.** The man must have patience and know it will take more time than wooing unattached single girls.

All three conditions apply to modern marketing. Two depend solely on the marketer's actions and one on the internal preconditions and predispositions of the client.

Physical Meeting

As in the *Kama Sutra*, the strongest attraction in marketing must start with a desire resulting from a *physical encounter* or from a *vision* (either with the product itself or through its advertising).

Approach

Location and timing. Meetings are occasions when lovers and beloved can be together. As mentioned, the buyer can encounter the brand in advertising, on the shelf, inside the store, on the Internet, and through word of mouth.

Meetings can be organized by the marketer or by intermediaries whenever or wherever the organization wants to enhance the actual brand contact with the personal touch. One of the most important encounters comes at a later stage, upon actual brand usage: The courted wife should not be left alone after she buys the brand. Someone from the wooing organization should try to reach her after, or while, she uses the brand, ready to answer questions, explain, and reinforce.

Meetings: spontaneous or planned. Spontaneous meetings need not be completely spontaneous; even spontaneous meetings can be planned:

> *"Meetings may be spontaneous or planned" (328).*

> "Meetings near the home can be accidental, but are often intentional. In a friend's house, while visiting a neighbor, at weddings, etc., they are the results of planning" "Best of all is the dwelling of a known and trusted go-between" (328).

This is where the Tupperware distribution was successful: in the residence of an interested host.

> *"By seeing her frequently he manages to win her confidence" (331).*

"Thus by means of constant attention over a long time, to the knowledge of all, he ends by being accepted" (331).

Vision

"A vision gives rise to a desire, which takes hold of the mind and becomes an obsession. She can no longer sleep, her body weakens, and she loses interest in everything, loses all sense of propriety, loses her reason, loses consciousness, and ends by dying." (310) This may be exaggerated for marketing, but I am sure the reader personally knows more than one (woman or man) shopper who follows some of the above steps.

Stronger Desire

"Although they are both in the same state, the feeling is stronger in the woman" (312).

Women will hardly leave their warm nest with the old, recognized, and secure brand if they do not develop an especially strong desire for the new brand. In marketing, the ideal transaction is when the client desires to buy the particular brand even more than the marketer cares to sell. How do you motivate the client—the wife of your competitor—to so eagerly desire to try your brand? This is where the Marketing Mix and the Love Mix strategies enter the picture. Public relations, advertising and product design, and word-of-mouth make existing brands obsolete, and Sensory Mixes inside the store create new sensations and desires.

Patience

If marketers really want to chase other men's wives, then time, patience, and consistency are needed: "Approached many a time and oft, she eventually gives way" (312).

Every-Monday Mike. While studying for my MBA at UCLA, I was assigned a project that required interviewing small- to medium-size manufacturers. One of my colleagues, as luck would have it, was a student who had worked for years as a salesman of basic chemicals for the leather industry. His sales territory was in downtown Los Angeles. We decided to interview some of his clients. One morning as we were walking around, he pointed out a certain factory, telling me the following fascinating story:

> This factory used to be one of my best clients for quite a few years. One day I found that, without any prior warning, they had switched to a new competitor. I approached the CEO's secretary, trying to analyze the reasons for this switch and discovered that nothing was wrong with our prices, the quality of our products, or our service. The secretary's story goes like this:
>
> "A year ago, one Monday morning, a new salesman appeared in the door. Dressed in a three-piece suit with a large smile on his face, he entered our office telling us his name is Mike and that he didn't come to sell anything since he knows how satisfied we are with our current supplier. But since he is new in the area, he was just dropping by to introduce himself, and he left his business card with me and with my boss. So he did every Monday morning at the same hour for a whole year. Stopping by, saying 'Hi,' telling a joke, and going on. One Monday, my boss noticed that Mike hadn't visited us for two weeks. The boss asked me to call his office, only to find out that Mike was hospitalized with minor surgery. My boss went to visit him, found out that they play golf at the same club, and so they became friends."
>
> And this is how I lost this client. Consistent repetition with patience and a smile did the selling job.

Chapter Five

On the Importance of Conversations

Women's conversations are such an important source of information and a vehicle for reaching women's emotions that their value must be emphasized again. Women have a strong need to converse about their experiences, especially to clarify vague or foggy issues and situations.

Conversation with a woman fulfills three needs: her need for information, her need to share with others, and your need to learn about her emotional structure and needs.

Conversations should start by talking to her concerning nothing in particular. Women are very quickly caught up in the vortex of a discussion, especially when one praises their ability and presence of mind.

Consulting

"When she consults him about some transaction, he explains how she should go about it. And then he declares she is wonderful and clever, which facilitates relations" (332).

This really means that, in connection with purchases, he gets the girl used to consulting him.

Conversation

In order to attract other men's wives, the author of the *Kama Sutra* indicates the importance of intimate talk (conversation) that could be activated either on the Web or in person. "They must first get acquainted and then speak. It is by talking together that they can appreciate their feelings and understand their mutual attitudes" (343). She will of course he is wooing someone else. "During their conversation, she must determine the boy's state of mind, to find out if he is interested in another" (342).

Difficulties with Bold Response

"Often those who refuse have already lost their innocence. They make difficulties only with words" (328). Marketers should remember that the mere fact that a wife of another organization is ready to listen to them is a sign of a potential affair. Vatsyayana recommends that if she is difficult and raises objections, "One must speak boldly to her without reserve, when she accepts the encounter" (328). The whole process is a serious one. Confronted with such seriousness, marketers should approach the woman with boldness—directly and straight to the point.

Women's Changeability

"A woman's nature is even more changeable than a man's, which is why they are inconsistent in their deeds and words" (344), but in spite of those difficulties, marketers should be constantly alert, because human nature is always changeable, especially among women.

Chapter Six

The Size of the Brand Sisterhood (Brand Harem)

Marketers should treat wives, either their own or their competition's, differently than just any regular buyer. Those wives should be assembled in a separate division headed by a separate manager—the so-called brand sisterhood.

Much More Than a Club

Knowing each other's secrets, harem women are bound together.
(382)

Some organizations will be tempted to call such a group by the trivial, worn-out name of some sort of customers' club: Silver Club, Diamond Club, or Platinum Club. However, this division is much more than any club. It is a special group in which the marketer can emotionally unite with his customers wives and where the customers as a group generate strength and deeper understanding of how the organization really satisfies their needs.

The brand sisterhood should be a very dignified sisterhood, cherished and difficult to join. The only difference between the king's harem and the brand's sisterhood is that in the latter, the more wives it has, the better each one feels: "With a woman whose nature one knows and with whom feelings are reciprocal, whatever one possesses is shared: everything is held in common" (332). In the former, the more wives it has, the less chance the king has for satisfying each, forcing the king to resort to artificial techniques.

Servicing Larger Brand Sisterhoods

The addition of other brands' wives would naturally increase the size of the brand sisterhood, demanding special attention from the marketer. One possibility is to utilize the internal strength and opportunities of the group

Internal satisfaction. It is only natural that marketers would raise the question of "How on earth we could satisfy all?" The answer to this question was also found in the ancient text: "There is only one husband, while the wives, who are often several, therefore remain unsatisfied. This is why, in practice, they have to obtain their satisfaction among themselves" (376). If you can't satisfy all simultaneously, then let them create satisfaction among themselves.

In Kama Sense Marketing, this analogy should guide marketers in developing their harem into a powerful, united, proud, and very satisfied group of lover-clients. With good understanding of natural feminine culture, marketers could develop internal communication schemes inside the sisterhood, through which women could discuss, converse, compare, and consult with other sisterhood members. Intimate blogs and forums, through which women can create their own language relating to the category and the brand, could be utilized to benefit both the organization and its valued clients. (In ancient China fifteen hundred years ago, women used the Nu Shu, a secret language known only to women, from which they generated much strength.)

Artificial love tricks. Marketers should do everything in their power to avoid resorting to artificial love tricks. For example, ancient times, the larger his harem, the more tricks the king had to use: "Out of kindliness, the king, although he had absolutely no wish to copulate, would fix to himself an artificial sex organ, thanks to which he alone in a single night could sleep with many women.... This is an old trick" (377). Marketers should be careful not to fall into this trap. But how should marketers run such large harems without resorting to artificial love tricks?

The answer is in proper planning, transparent reciprocal love, smart use of IT and data mining, and efficient use of the Internet.

In Sum: Learn to Protect Your Wife

The masters explain that, as far as sexual matters are concerned, the harem must be protected. (385)

Listening for clues. One way for marketers to protect their wives is to track their messages on the web forums and blogs, as recommended two thousand years ago. "According to Babhravyas, one must listen to the gossip of other women, especially those who dissimulate their behavior, so as to be able to judge the morality or immorality of one's wives" (385).

Predicting at-risk behavior. Organizations should learn, in their customer-satisfaction models, how to identify and predict ahead of time when their wives are at risk of switching to other brands. "The six causes of corruption in women are drinking, contact with corrupt men, absence of the husband on a trip abroad, dreams, changes of residence, and physical suffering inflicted" (387).

Action—Part Five

Embarking on the road to adultery is a difficult march (journey). In order to succeed you need extensive research, careful planning, and continuous wooing.

1. Start with dedicated, specific research. Study the frequency, size, and vulnerability of your target (other brands') wives, using small cells, limited population, and mostly qualitative research. Emphasize heavy users or loyalists of the different brands in a particular category. When you commission regular research, study large enough samples of those low-incidence groups, regardless of cost. *Look for the coin where it fell and not under the light.* In some goods, especially in the FMCG, use in-store point-of-purchase interviewing methods for assessing:

1. the number of other brands' wives who are potential switchers and

2. the emotional factors that affect the behavior of other organizations' wives who have visited your shelf or store.

Use these interviews to help assess the risk of time and money involved and, even more so, to decide on which brands' wives you will concentrate first.

Note: Attracting wives of a large competitor may require a different emotional strategy than attracting wives of a smaller one. For example, a customer coming from a small bank is already accustomed to a personal and quiet atmosphere of doing business, while a customer of a large bank is by nature interested more in strength, stability, and a solid base.

2. Develop and use an Adultery Index. Consider developing a susceptibility index: the Adultery Index. Based on the *Kama Sutra*, such an index could measure the following:

- How strong is her love for her existing brand (commitment)?
- Has she had a negative experience with her current (competitive) brand? If so, how deep is her dissatisfaction?
- Is she preoccupied with other issues and therefore unable currently to meet other brands?
- Does she perceive herself as being contractually free from her existing brand (especially true in banking, insurance, cellular phones, etc.)?
- How does she perceive the image and attributes of the wooing brand (especially financially secured, big, innovative, or conservative)?
- Has she had previous encounters with the wooing brand? Were these encounters positive or negative?
- Are there any ethical reasons that can prevent or stop such an affair?

As a precaution, track regularly the Adultery index of your own wives in order to detect vulnerable spots in advance.

3. Decide on your marriage and adultery targets. Do you prefer to concentrate more on keeping your existing loyal wives from switching to other competitor's brands or wooing other brands' wives? If both, in what proportions? Or do you prefer to attract new occasional buyers?

Note: Even if you decide to restrict your activities to your existing customers (infrequent or loyal wives), you may find other brands' wives joining you through positive rumors circulating about your existing wives, as well as their word-of-mouth recommendations.

If those new wives happen to be chronic switchers, you may reject them yourself.

Note: If you decide to pursue other brands' wives, be ready for a very difficult and time-consuming task. Carefully plan and budget for mainly personal and interactive approaches, including assigning a special task force for locating, courting, and attracting those other wives.

4. Create a well-defined and well-budgeted strategy based on a well-thought-out research plan, since each of the competitors' loyal wives may be worth more to you than ten regular or infrequent buyers.

Hint: Do not expect regular advertising to do the job. Your existing wives' word of mouth could be more powerful if directed properly.

5. Before buying databases of category users, conduct a pilot test on a small sample to indicate the vulnerability of such a list. For example, you can send sample list members an emotional teaser in a direct approach and see what proportion responds positively.

6. Make sure your staff, at all contact points, is sensitive to a potential switcher and ready with the right issue and discussion points. The mere fact that another organization's wife is ready to listen to your courting is by itself a sign of a potential affair.

7. Fine-tune your Sensory Mix for the first encounter. Making sure your Sensory Mix is optimal, carefully prepare the other brand's wife's first encounter with your brand or staff. Physical meetings are best; you can then present your brand, staff, and philosophy in one encounter.

Note: Wives of other brands may have already developed and received many positive sensory experiences from the other brand.

Therefore, they may expect some sophistication in your Sensory Mix.

8. Decide on the kind of sisterhood you wish to develop with your wives and to which you will invite other organization's wives. Is it a physical place or just virtual (as in the Web)?

9. Keep wooing. Continue to give her the feeling that you care for her after you have seduced her. Make sure that she is actively interacting with your existing wives. Make use of the internal power of the sisterhood. Always be ready to approach, refer to, and treat each new wife personally.

10. Encourage the formation of a unique online community of women lovers of the brand. This community would inform, converse, and share everything that has to do with using the brand and the lifestyle surrounding or associated with its use. Try to convert this community into a physical one, where women will meet among themselves or with the producers and marketers of the brand, as well as with newly arrived users.

11. Develop alternative conversation scenarios to help online meetings be efficient and productive. Some should be bold, without reserve, such as: "I realize that you are very happy with [competitive brand], and we quite appreciate this. We are very envious of [competitive brand] for having such a customer! You are very important to us, and we will do everything we can to bring you to try [our brand]."

12. Since it is hard to reach your competitors' wives, resort to the use of knitworking:

- Some of your wives are natural advocates of your brand; give them the right stage for exercising their natural desire.
- Develop a women mentoress within your organization who understands women's language and knows how to

flatter a woman. She will lead the way and train your staff for better understanding of your wives' needs (see part 6).

13. Develop Conversation Circles. Use ethnographic and qualitative research to find the conversation triggers and ways category users interact between themselves. Those issues could be described in circles around the brand. In the closest circle are topics related to the physical benefits of the brand. In the next circle, there could be topics related to the whole category; the next circle could refer to the emotional benefits; the next circle to general related issues; and finally, the women's state of mind in relation to the category.

Part Six

On Choosing a Female Mentor
(On Courtesans)

It is always easy to find male instructors [of Kama Sutra practices],
but in the case of girls, it is not at all easy to find one for erotic arts.
This is why Vatsyayana finds it simpler to advise that women should
teach this subject, so long as they are trustworthy and well-born.
(51)

Part 6, the second largest part of the ancient book, is devoted to
the role of professional women and attests to their importance
in those days. The ancient book describes a whole spectrum of
professional women in the arts of love; however, I have found
one of those to be the most intriguing: the courtesan.

The Role of Courtesans

In Indian society, courtesans have always been respected, not only
for their beauty, their way of life, and their attraction, but also for
their knowledge, their usefulness, and their social role. (50)

As mentioned, most marketers are men. Few really know the
secrets of women's language and culture or their true needs as
women or customers. Rare are such talented men as Mr. Mouro,
head of the first large department store in nineteenth-century
Paris, in Émile Zola's *The Ladies' Paradise*. This department store
catered only to women from the upper-middle class. Mr. Mouro,
a very successful womanizer, understood the secrets of women's
needs and culture and knew how to converse with women, making
him irresistible in both purchase and sex. He could seduce any
woman or make her buy his merchandise.

However, most modern managers need the help of female
mentors, either as employees or as consultants, to convey
emotional messages to women married to other brands. Only
expert women could help male marketers develop the marriage
or the sisterhood strategies discussed in part 5.

In ancient times, courtesans performed those duties. They knew perfectly how to make the most of the feminine secrets and the arts of love. "Unrivaled in singing, music, dancing, declamation, appearance, and eroticism, courtesans were set in the three worlds by the creator" (420). Being so, they held a superior position as both consultants to men and as lovers. The ancient Hindus recognized courtesans as an important part of Oriental society and they were regarded with respect. Their education was superior to the average women; being better educated, they were more fun to be with.

Models of Feminine Behavior

> *In ancient times, princes and princesses were sent to courtesans to learn the arts and good manners.... Not only were the courtesans respected, but their presence brought good luck.... They are teachers of the arts of pleasure and music for the children of kings and nobles. (51)*

Modern love mentoresses. In the histories of the Buddhist Jatakas, the courtesans are cited as models of feminine behavior. Are such women missing in our modern society, especially when it comes to marketing and selling to women?

And my answer is, indeed yes! Those courtesans were rich in experiences and in the 64 arts of love. They reached their status in society because of their unique instincts and intuitions, qualities in short supply in the all-male professional community. When I carefully read of the courtesans' role, I realized they could be the modern business mentoress to the male managers, or what the Bible (Genesis 2:20) calls a "helpmeet."

Like research, conversation is of overriding importance in each segment of the marketing process. Yet we men do not understand conversation and gossip. We need a woman to help us understand conversation with our customers and make it genuine, true, and honest. If marketers wish to love their women employees or their female clients, there is no better mentor than those expert women—full of intuition, knowledge, and expertise in everything that surrounds emotionality and love.

Filling the Gap in Business School

Just as in the art of war, skill in managing arms is indispensable, so in the art of love, skill in technique and adaptability to all circumstances are also essential.(136)

Vatsyayana supports the importance of the woman's role as mentor: "A courtesan spends her assets on religious, cultural, or social enterprises. Being a high-class heroine, a courtesan has relations with heroes belonging to high society" (466).

"Courtesans are trained from childhood in the techniques of love and the ways of attracting men" (420), and until business schools start teaching the arts of love and gender marketing, we will have to resort to engaging expert feminine mentors who help men on feminine issues in Kama Sense.

Traits of a Successful Business Mentoress

The courtesan arouses desire, brings pleasure, inspires love, then goes away after devouring all the money of those she seduces.

A mentoress should be versed in all aspects of emotionality in the business world, both internally (with employees) and externally (with customers). In servicing the male marketers, here are some *Kama Sutra* behaviors that could enhance the business environment and be taught in coaching schools in business. Her major role should be to introduce the concept of how to love and be loved in the marketing environment:

- "Even though she is not the wife of one man alone, she binds herself to a steady lover. She should give him the feeling that he is her only lover" (405).
- "In order to please the hero to whom she is attached, she

behaves like a wife" (405). Therefore, a good mentoress should behave like his wife, servicing no competitors at the same time.

- "She praises the hero's virtues" (409).

In some countries, some top business executives and celebrities frequently consult experts in Kabala or other mystical pursuits. I wouldn't be surprised if behind those visits is a woman recommending or initiating such moves.

Outside Consultant Role

In order to maintain her prestige, she should never satisfy anyone without being paid for it. (392)

Love mentors should be no different from other business mentors in being paid well for their services, because if people don't pay the right amount they don't appreciate the service. These modern mentoresses should be outside consultants, able to move from one organization to another and ready to move on to the next client upon completing their task. Only an outside consultant could really free herself of the internal politics in each organization and express her intuitive and emotional creativity. She should come in only after the directors have been completely sold on this idea and are ready for the experience.

Action—Part Six

By now, you have decided on the type of women you wish to woo and eventually marry and determined the type of love and reciprocity you wish to pursue. Now, if you are a male marketer, and you quite agree that the emotional behavior of your female clients is a mystery, you must do the following.

1. **Decide on the type of mentoring you need** (depth of emotional process, type of women to woo, type of messages, etc.) and decide whether to assign a woman mentoress only to yourself, to your senior staff, or to all of those (sales and service) who come in contact with the client.

2. **Employ outside freelance consultants for relatively higher fees** rather than using an in-house employee, because:

- Good mentoresses are hard to find.
- A mentoress should be experienced in a variety of issues.
- Emotional knowledge is constantly changing.
- You may use different mentoresses for different assignments.

Part Seven

How to Tell Creative from Occult in Marketing

(Occult Practices)

If the desired results are not obtained by the means described up to this point, occult practices must be utilized. (489)

The *Kama Sutra* rather apologetically explains that part 7, "Occult Practices," is an appendix—an add-on that does not really belong to the original six-part manuscript. Yet in today's marketing, we often rely on "part 7" rather than engaging in the creative potential and efficacy of parts 1–6.

True Creativity versus Occult Practices

I know that half of my advertising dollars are wasted ... I just don't know which half.

Marketers and advertising experts very often cite the above quote by John Wanamaker, considered the father of modern advertising, at the end of the nineteenth century. But today, I am afraid, in many campaigns, the money is much more than half wasted. It is quite distressing indeed that even today, with all the available technology and scientific advances, professionals would still quote the same saying (or myth).

Wanamaker's myth is still with us today because marketers and advertising people refuse to make the delicate distinction between real creativity and occult, planning and improvising. In their efforts to draw attention, they search for

> **Wanamaker's myth is still with us today because...** marketers and advertising people do not make the delicate distinction between creative and magic.

any kind of new or surprising ingredients; they draw a lot of encouragement from the Marketing Mix theory, which defines the marketing expert as: "A mixer of ingredients, who sometimes follows a recipe as he goes along, sometimes adapts a recipe to the ingredients immediately available, and sometimes experiments with or invents ingredients no one else has tried."*

---

* Borden, Neil H., originator of the Marketing Mix concept (inspired by J. Culliton, 1949), *American Marketing Association* presidential address, 1953.

Creative Is Relevant

There is nothing wrong with the above efforts, as long as they have relevancy to the functional or the emotional benefits the customer expects from the brand. If, in the consumer's eyes, it has relevancy, then it is creative, and if the consumer sees no relevancy in it, then it is occult. In many cases, when we expose consumers of a particular category to advertising commercials after erasing the name of the sponsoring brand, we find that consumers, after viewing the commercial two or three times, do not remember the message, the product category, or the brand name.

Beauty, New, or Surprising versus Real, Deeper Benefits

In an effort to introduce order into the wilderness of occult practices, the ancient text tries to define boundaries for the occult: "Beauty, qualities, age, and generosity are the causes of success in love" (489). One of the ways to attract attention is by beauty, and young organizations may attract clients by emphasizing their sheer beauty and youth. They should invest in unique designs, energetic advertising, and unique promotional campaigns. (This observation is not to detract from the experience, sophistication, maturity, and trust of the older organizations.)

Yet the Kama Sense Marketing analogy is also very clear. Some marketers, in their quest for clients' love, resort only to beauty (the domain of the creative advertisers or product designers) and refrain from looking for real and deeper client benefits, either functional or emotional.

Compensating Occult Techniques

Occult practices are employed when the "real thing" fails or does not exist at all, as the following quote suggests: "If one is incapable of satisfying a passionate woman, techniques must be used" (508).

And Vatsyayana didn't mean just Viagra, but he also suggests a mix of ancient recipes: "Crush the flowers of pink lotus and blue lotus, mixed with snake's saffron. Let it dry. These ingredients consumed together with honey or ghee, make one attractive" (491).

> **In the absence of real creativity, we tend to look for refuge in the "occult"—the mystical or the magical.**
>
> **If such a campaign has any relevancy to the product's functional or emotional benefits, it could be considered creative, but if it lacks such relevancy, it is occult.**

Although its efficacy is difficult to prove, the above formula definitely has some relevancy to marketing. Not only because fifteen hundred years ago they have used the term *Ingredients* exactly as Neil Borden did in describing the meaning of the Marketing Mix in the twentieth century. It has relevancy because in modern marketing too, in the absence of real creativity, marketers may take refuge in the occult—the mystical or the magical ingredients. It is very common to see crazy TV commercials that would do anything to draw consumer attention, trying to arouse customers' feelings or to surprise them. If such a campaign has any relevancy to the product's functional or emotional benefits, it could be considered creative, but if it lacks such relevancy, it is occult.

The *Kama Sutra* would not stop at anything in proposing such occult ideas: "By holding in one's left hand a peacock's or hyena's eye, wrapped in gold, one finds success in love" (491). If a modern art director would use such a visual in order to sell "eye cleaners" to human beings, or maybe optical lenses to older peacocks, then it could definitely be considered a creative campaign because it is relevant. But if, God forbid, it is used to draw attention to a particular fashion, to an avant garde car, or maybe to cottage cheese or a new yogurt, it should be categorized as occult and not relevant. Such a campaign definitely does not connote love to its customers, since it is not integrated into the needs, mood, character, and lifestyle of the people who use the product.

Occult and superficial. Some years ago, I was called upon by one of Israel's largest electrical power concerns to present results of a recent survey. The agency director then presented his ideas for a new campaign—supposedly based on my research findings. I was shocked to discover the campaign had been offered to another client in a completely different category three months before. After the presentation, the director approached me rather secretly to explain that they had invested so much in preparing this campaign for the previous client, who had rejected it, that they would hate to see this money go down the drain. This, in my opinion, is occult and superficial.

Obesity and fruit yogurt. A yogurt manufacturer decided to launch a large advertising campaign positioning his fruit yogurt as a fun and sexy product with lots of very obese people singing and dancing in the streets. Are fun, obesity, and sex relevant to fruit yogurt? If the answer is yes, then this could be considered as good and creative advertising. But, if the answer is no, then it is sheer occult.

Creativity with Care and Ethics

Magic practices are forbidden, because they destroy trust and the feeling of security. (280)

Creative possibilities are endless. Marketers should not stop at any new or even ancient idea to arouse their clients, but they should do it with extreme care and ethics. All of those occult practices, in my opinion, are not sufficient for promoting the first encounter with your customer.

> Marketers should not stop at any new or even ancient idea to arouse their clients, but they should do it with extreme care and ethics.

Qualities and Generosity

Generosity makes everyone more likable, whether one is ugly, stupid, or old.

Beauty and age are obvious advantages, but in their absence, generosity could compensate. When the organization tries genuinely to bestow generosity upon its clients, it can overcome age and lack of beauty. The mere fact that generosity appears here interestingly suggests that discounts, prizes, and price reductions—by themselves—could easily be viewed by consumers as occult practices for obtaining love.

Occult Techniques to Satisfy Many

Crush vidari roots in cow's milk, together with svayamagupta seeds, sugar, honey, and ghee. Use it to make biscuits with wheat flour. He who eats them, as many as suits him, can enjoy an unlimited number of women, the ancient masters tell us.(501)

We accept that salespeople constantly try to woo all customers who enter the store because they don't have a way to recognize and cater to the serious customers. The phony sales smile and the "May I help you?" border on being occult practices of reaching out to the masses instead of targeting the loving consumer.

How can we make the selling process more efficient and make the customer love us? It would be nice if she would enter the store and say, "I want to buy shoes; please make my life simple." We would then ask her size and point her to an appropriate selection on the shelf.

Instead, the customer says, "Leave me alone. I just want to walk around. I love shopping." Shopping is a way of life for most of our customers. This is part of women's culture. The sales staff must accept the customer's "shopping" without doing something negative, such as nagging her. They must observe the customer from a distance and approach her only when she really needs a salesperson.

Here, occult techniques may be of great help. One can easily envision using magical formulas in modern advertising to deliver subliminal secrets to naive customers. Perhaps organizations should refrain from giving such formulas to their salespeople!

Maintaining Balance

In love, not all kinds of action can be practiced at all times with all women. In amorous practices, the man's behavior should take into account the place, the country, and the moment.(167)

In both romantic and marketing love, emotional relationships require a harmony between passion, emotion, and logic. Our ultimate goal as marketers is to deal deeply with the few. We must find ways to sift through the customers to find the loving wives.

In doing so, we must always uphold the basic philosophy that man must select techniques and procedures that remain within the province of virtue and love: "He who wishes to preserve virtue, wealth, and love in this world and in the next must have a thorough knowledge of this treatise and, at the same time, master his senses [and] ... establish a stable marriage" (521).

Action—Part Seven

1. Use occult only as a final resort. You can try your luck with occult practices if your honest and genuine wooing efforts do not work.

2. Be particularly conscientious. Once in a while, you may throw some magical practices into your Marketing Mix activities, and especially into your advertising activities, in addition to your functional and emotional strategies. But you should always make sure that the majority of your mix is real, transparent, ethical, and genuine.

3. Are you perceived as a young or old organization? Conduct the right research to indicate your emotional profile (brand assets) among your customers. For example, if you are an old and established organization, are you perceived by your customers as experienced, sophisticated, mature, solid, and trustworthy or as conservative, slow to react, and reluctant to change?

4. Relevancy is the real test. Everything else is occult. Always try to test your many creative ideas, especially in your promotion, for relevancy. Ask your potential customers if the idea makes sense to them and if they find it relevant to their emotional or functional needs.

Appendix I

Step-by-Step Kama Sense Marketing

Here's a bird's-eye view of how to move from your current marketing approaches to Kama Sense Marketing success.

From Emotional to Love Marketing

Rule 1: Don't beat around the bush. Enter the world of love through the front door. If you truly seek emotional satisfaction for customers, you must include love in your marketing strategies and mission statements.

From One-Sided Love to Fully Reciprocal Love

Rule 2: Don't be a spectator. Love starts from within. Love of the consumer should be initiated by the organization and not vice versa. The organization must also love its employees; if the employees don't love the organization and its brands, they won't be able to love its customers.

From Non-Gender Marketing to Male–Female Courting

Rule 3: Woo the customer. Although women make or influence 85 percent of the household buying decisions, most marketers are male. This creates a sort of disguised courtship between the marketer and the customer.

From Marketing Mix to Love Mix

Rule 4: The wooing never ends. Preludes (before the purchase) and Conclusions (after the purchase) form part of the act of love. The Love Mix starts when the Marketing Mix ends. The wooing process never ends.

From Sight and Sound to Full-Sense Marketing

Rule 5: Give more than two senses' worth. The more senses your products and marketing trigger in your customers, the more attached your customers will feel to your products. A "Sensory Star" helps visualize how to strategize the unique sensory mix for each product; the soul is added as a sixth sense.

From Flat to 64 Sources of Inspiration

Rule 6: Draw on a wealth of tried-and-true arts. If you genuinely adopt the attitude that you love your customers, you will more correctly use the 64 arts to show this love and woo them. The 64 tried-and-true arts provide a wealth of ideas that can inspire creative and successful marketing.

From Complacency to a Serious After Play

Rule 7: Design an extensive BUYER program. A lot of attention should be given to the way your customer is using the product and the experience she gets from it.

From Aloof to Vow Taking

Rule 8: Marry the customer. This is the purpose of Kama Sense Marketing—to marry the customer. This is a cognitive, intellectual moment in the middle of an emotional process. However, not all customers are worth marrying.

From Marketing Rules to Instinct and Intuition

Rule 9: Promote mentoresses. Modern organizations must grant women executive positions in all areas that involve emotions and teamwork (including marketing, human resources, and many others). Female marketers will be the "big sisters"—the mentors of both male managers and female consumers. Women should not try to imitate men. Organizations will eventually learn to utilize feminine power to their advantage.

From Occult to Creative in Marketing

Rule 10: Always check relevancy. If your advertising is relevant, it is creative. If it is not, it may be occult.

Appendix II

The Sixty-four Arts of Love

Waiting for creative marketers to be activated in their Sensory Mix strategy as described in Richard Burton's translation of the original Kama Sutra: "The following are the arts to be studied, together with the Kama Sutra" (p83-86)

1. Singing

2. Playing on musical instruments

3. Dancing

4. Union of dancing, singing and playing instrumental music

5. Writing and drawing

6. Tattooing

7. Arraying and adorning an idol with rice and flowers

8. Spreading and arranging beds or couches of flowers

9. Coloring the teeth, garments, hair, nails, and bodies

10. Fixing stained glass into a floor

11. The art of making beds, and spreading out carpets and cushions for reclining

12. Playing on musical glasses filled with water

13. Storing and accumulating water in aqueducts and reservoirs

14. Picture making, trimming, and decorating

15. Stringing of rosaries, necklaces, garlands, and wreaths

16. Binding of turbans and chaplets

17. Scenic representations, stage playing

18. Art of making ear ornaments

19. Art of preparing perfumes and odours

20. Proper disposition of jewels, decorations, and adornment in dress

21. Magic or sorcery

22. Quickness of hand or manual skills

23. Culinary art

24. Making lemonades, sherbets , acidulated drinks

25. Tailor's work and sewing

26. Making parrots, flowers, tufts, tassels, etc out of yarn or thread

27. Solutions of riddles, enigmas, covert speeches, verbal puzzles and enigmatical question

28. A game in repeating verses

29. The art of mimicry or imitation

30. Reading, including chanting and intoning

31. Study of sentences difficult to pronounce

32. Practice with sword ....and bow and arrow

33. Drawing inferences, reasoning or inferring

34. Carpentry

35. Architecture, or the act of building

36. Knowledge about gold or silver coins, and jewels and gems

37. Chemistry and mineralogy

38. Colouring jewels, gems and beads

39. Gardening

40. Art of cock fighting, quail fighting and ram fighting

41. Art of teaching parrots and starlings to speak

42. Art of applying perfumed ointments to the body

43. The art of understanding writing in cipher

44. The art of speaking by changing the forms of words

45. Knowledge of language and of the vernacular dialects

46. Art of making flower carriages

47. Art of framing mystical diagrams and addressing spells

48. Mental exercises

49. Composing poems

50. Knowledge of dictionaries and vocabularies

51. Knowledge of ways of changing and disguising the appearance of persons

52. Knowledge of the art of changing the appearance of things

53. Various ways of gambling

54. Art of obtaining possession of the property of others

55. Skill in youthful sports

56. Knowledge of the rules of society, and how to pay respect and compliments to others

57. Knowledge of the art of war, of arms, of armies, etc.

58. Knowledge of gymnastics

59. Art of knowing the character of a man from his features

60. Knowledge of scanning or constructing verses

61. Arithmetical recreations

62. Making artificial flowers

63. Making figures and images in clay